Cacti in New Mexico

by New Mexico Agricultural Experiment Station

with an introduction by Roger Chambers

Self Reliance Books

Get more historic titles on animal and stock breeding, gardening and old fashioned skills by visiting us at:

http://selfreliancebooks.blogspot.com/

Introduction

I am pleased to present yet another title on Ginseng.

The work is in the Public Domain and is re-printed here in accordance with Federal Laws.

As with all reprinted books of this age that are intended to perfectly reproduce the original edition, considerable pains and effort had to be undertaken to correct fading and sometimes outright damage to existing proofs of this title. At times, this task is quite monumental, requiring an almost total "rebuilding" of some pages from digital proofs of multiple copies. Despite this, imperfections still sometimes exist in the final proof and may detract from the visual appearance of the text.

I hope you enjoy reading this book as much as I enjoyed making it available to readers again.

Roger Chambers

OPUNTIA CLAVATA.   Showing habit of growth.

OPUNTIA CLAVATA

INTRODUCTION.

There are two concepts more or less closely associated in the minds of a large number of people in New Mexico, both of which are in some degree inaccurate and which need correction before we can discuss the subject of this bulletin. The first is that any queer looking spiny plant found growing wild on the mesa or in the mountains is a cactus; and the second is that New Mexico is the home of the cactus. It therefore becomes necessary to state pretty definitely just what a cactus is so the reader may understand what we are talking about in the bulletin. The correction if the other idea is easier and of less relative importance to our purpose.

CHARACTERISTICS OF THE CACTI.

In the classification of plants botanists are practically agreed in the belief that similarity of flower structures indicates much closer relationship than any other kind of similarity, and since they assume that plants are genetically related and try to express that relationship in the arrangement of them in principal and subsidary groups, it naturally follows that they associate plants having the same group of flower characters in families; and resemblances in plan of structure of flowers are accepted as having much more fundamental significance than similarities of individual organs, especially the vegetative ones (i. e. the organs concerned in the nutrition or growing of the plant). Hence it is that the botanist will assemble apparently rather diverse plants in the same family because of similarity of flower structure not readily appreciated by the ordinary observer.

The cacti of New Mexico have flowers with the following characteristics: They are mostly large for the plant, varying from about one-half an inch to fully four inches long in the different species. The calyx consists of from one to several rows of more or less fleshy or waxy sepals united at the base and attached to the top of the ovary. In the outer row the sepals are usually slightly greenish, somewhat like sepals of other kinds of flowers, but the inner ones gradually change into the delicate waxy petals of which there are ordinarily two or sometimes more whorls, and these are united at the base with the sepals forming a more or less elongated tube. Inside the tube are the very numerous stamens, 100 or more, each with a 2-celled anther on a slender filament. The ovary is under all the other parts of the flower seeming to be imbedded in a peculiarly modified stem, at least in some of the genera. It has many ovules which become the seeds in the dry or leathery or fleshy, berry-like fruit. The styles are united into a single stout one and the stigmas are usually separate, there being from 5 to a dozen or more.

Besides the characteristics of the flower just discussed the structure of the plant body of the cacti is distinctly different from that of most plants and so peculiar as to attract attention from almost everyone. It has several characteristics which fit it especially for life in an arid region, in fact nearly all its most characteristic peculiarities are in some way connected with adaptation to arid land conditions.

The leaf surface is reduced to nothing at all in all but a few genera, but the fact that one sub-trophical genus has persistent foliar though thickened fleshy leaves, which function as all leaves do, and another genus (*Opuntia*) has rudimentary leaves that never function and soon fall off, indicates that the family has acquired the leafless habit in response to the conditions under which it has lived. Since leaves naturally furnish transpiration surface and transpiration is a process resulting in the loss of water, the reduction of leaf surface would naturally reduce the amount of water lost by the plant and therefore reduce the amount of water necessary for the plant in order that it might live.

The nearer a body approaches a spherical form the less surface does it have in proportion to its solid content or volume. When a plant has lost its leaves, transpiration must go on through its stem surface, for some transpiration must take place in all land plants. The desirable, from the standpoint of a plant living in a arid region, is that the *minimum amount* of transpiration should occur; hence the thickening of the stems is but another means of reducing transpiration surface.

Two other methods of still further reducing the loss of water are seen in the cacti. The epidermis of the plant (the outside layer or "skin") is much thickened and hardened on the outer surface making the cells more resistent to the loss of water from the succulent tissues within; and the sap is not watery as in many plants but is mucilaginous, thus tending to hold the water, as well as quickly sealing any accidental break in the epidermis.

The thickened stem is advantageous in another way, since it offers a relatively large storage capacity for moisture when the plant is able to get water.

Attention has been called to the fact that desert plants usually have relatively large root systems spreading either deep into the ground where the water table is only a few feet down, or spreading widely just below the surface where the ground water is entirely out of reach. The cacti belong in the latter category and their roots are long and slender (sometimes tuberous thickened) and cover relatively large areas about the plants. In this way they are able to collect water from a large area (for desert plants do not stand thickly over the ground as do plants of the moist regions) and a very small amount of rainfall is sufficient to give such plants a refreshing drink. This arrangement also makes possible the rapid absorption of moisture when there is plenty, a factor of great importance in the arid region where the precipitation is mostly torrential in character. That animals eat plants goes without saying, and that such succulent plants as cacti would be especially palatable to a thirsty animal is self-evident; hence the spiny defence that is so efficient.

Thus we see the cacti are abundantly fitted to collect water rapidly when there is abundance; make the most of a small supply; and utilize most effectively whatever they get by being practically immune to the effects of the most rigorous drought, and at the same time be amply protected from the attacks of hungry and thirsty animals.

Plants that are able to grow rapidly bloom profusely, and mature seed in a short "rainy season" and that can edure a "dry season" are sometimes called trophophytes, and most of the tropical plants are to some extent of this character. Plants able to endure extremely dry conditions are known as xerophytes and the cacti are certainly of this kind. But considered as a family, they are also somewhat tropophytic. The New Mexican species have adapted themselves to the endurance of great daily and annual range of temperature, another very unfavorable climatic condition.

GEOGRAPHICAL DISTRIBUTION.

Attention has been called, in another place,* to the climatic requirements of the cacti, and it has been shown that they are adapted to a region where the temperature is moderately high but not excessive; where the minimum temperature is not very low (many species will endure continued and severe freezing, but by far the greater number will not); and where the rainfall is periodic and moderate in amount with long periods of drought between. The region of the Western Hemisphere having climatic conditions such as these is the one occupied by the CACTACEAE or cactus family. A similar region in Africa is occupied by an entirely different family of plants (the Spurges) which has developed a structure of plant body similar to that of the cacti, but whose flower characters are very different.

As is intimated by the above, the cactus family is native on the American continents, the species now growing in the old world having been introduced from this hemisphere. Its extreme limits of distribution are those of the land in the Western hemisphere, there being at least some representatives, mostly more than one, all the way from Alaska to Patagonia. The genus most widely distributed and apparently most able to adapt itself to varying climatic conditions is *Opuntia*.

The latest treatment of the CACTACEAE† (a German book) divides the family into 21 genera and lists about 700 species that it was possible to recognize from the literature and the specimens available to the author for study. There are apparently two centers of distribution, one in each of the American continents. The greater number of species and individual plants are found in North America with the center of this distribution area in the State of San Luis Potosi, Mexico. From this region the number of genera, and individuals if not species, diminishes as one travels northward, so that by the time New Mexico is reached these plants have become a relatively subordinate part of the vegetation, and attract attention not so much by their abundance as by their strik-

---

*Bull. 60, New Mexico Experiment Station, page 29.
†Schumann. Gesamtbeschreibung der Kakteen.

ing differences from other and much more common plants that posesses characteristics we are accustomed to. As considered in this paper there are five genera of cacti represented in New Mexico, and sixty-three species are here listed. Of three of these species the author has not seen material from New Mexico. One of the three is common at El Paso and we have material from there growing in the cactus garden. The other two are reported from New Mexico in the original descriptions and one is described from plants collected in New Mexico. Of the 63 species mentioned we have 48 under cultivation in the cactus garden and are acquainted with several of the others as they grow in the field. In the preparation of this paper the author has had access to the preserved material in the U. S. National Herbarium which is particularly rich in cactus specimens, since Dr. Rose has been collecting material in this family for a number of years. The author has been studying, collecting, and growing them since 1904.

CLIMATIC CONDITIONS.

In a general way the climatic conditions of New Mexico are not favorable to the cacti. It is either too cold or too dry or both for most of the species. At the lower levels, where the weather is hot enough to make them grow well during the summer season, the minimum temperature in the winter is too low for many species and the amount of water which falls is entirely inadequate for the requirements of even more species, notwithstanding the current opinion that cacti will grow "on the top of the stove or on one's office desk."

The author once collected two plants in the early spring and threw them on the floor behind the stove to dry out, expecting to use them as herbarium specimens. Over a month later both specimens bloomed. But this does not mean that the plants do not require water to grow. It simply means that they are able to retain the water they get for a long time and use it most economically in the production of flowers and seeds. The species found growing in New Mexico are those which either can live on a very small amount of water (and, therefore, grow very slowly and attain only a relatively small size), or can edure severe winter temperatures.

To give some definite idea of climatic conditions which the plants must endure in New Mexico it is only necessary to say that the *minimum* temperature (which is the most important temperature

factor governing plant distribution) is higher than 7° to 10° F.
(20° to 25° below freezing) nowhere in the state, with periodic low
minimums of about 0° F. for even the warmest places. The cold-
est localities are subject to temperatures many degrees below 0° F.
Elizabethtown (altitude over 8,000 feet) reports 20° or more
below 0° F. every winter, and even Roswell has a record of-29° F.
While these low temperatures may not occur every year, the plants
naturally distribute themselves over an area so slowly that these
low temperatures occuring at long intervals are still sufficient to
keep species that cannot endure them out of the region entirely.

The precipitation in New Mexico varies with the locality from
less than 8 inches (probably as low as 6 inches) to probably over
30 inches. But the low precipitation is coupled with the warmer
temperatures and the greater precipitation with the colder temperatures, hence the necessary moderately abundant precipitation and
high temperature do not anywhere occur together.

And it naturally follows that only those species which are able
to endure these extreme conditions will grow in New Mexico at
all. It is even doubtful whether species which grow in the foothills up to 5,500 feet elevation at the southern end of the state
will grow on the plains or in the mountains at similar or higher elevations in the northern end. Certain it is that they do not do so
now with absolutely nothing to limit their distribution except the
prevailing climatic conditions. And yet we have been told that the
thornless cactus is to make the deserts produce an almost unlimited
forage crop.

USES OF CACTI.

With the commercial exploitation of the spineless or thornless
cactus—of which certainly nearly everyone has heard by this time
—there arose a demand for more definite and authoritative information on the subject of the economic value of these plants in
New Mexico and work has been carried on along several lines
to bring together all that is known or could be found out in regard
to them. Such great claims had been made for them that many
people were interested and several private individuals and experiment station workers and U. S. Department of Agriculture special-
ists attacked the subject, each in his own field and from his own
personal point of view. In the past seven years a large amount of

work has been done and much has been published on the subject. The subject has been shown to be a very large one, the bounds of which are not yet appreciated.

Dr. David Griffiths of the U. S. Department of Agriculture has, no doubt, made the most exhaustive study in the field and his results have been published in bulletins issued by the Bureau of Plant Industry, Bureau of Animal Industry and Office of Experiment Stations. The Experiment Station workers of California, Arizona, Texas, and New Mexico have all been working at some phase of the subject and have published more or less about it. The work has taken the form of investigations of the plants in their natural habitats, cultivation under garden and field conditions, feeding tests, chemical studies of the plants and fruits; and preliminary breeding work has been done by a number of investigators. The commercial exploitations of the spineless forms has gone on in California, though with hardly the success prophesied and expected even by the dealers themselves.

The literature on this subject published by the Department of Agriculture and the Experiment Stations is restrained, carefully exact in expression, and rests on experiments performed; it is always conservative in its estimates and it prophesies are "safe."

Much of the advertising literature scattered broad-cast through the arid Southwest is incorrect in actual statement and leads to much more inaccurate generalization, especially in the hands of people who have just come into the arid region from the states farther east. The advertisers of the spineless species but made a common mistake when they assumed that because their plants would grow well in southern California in a region where oranges do well, that region being a "desert," therefore their plants would grow any place and equally well in the desert regions from California to Texas and north to Nevada and Utah. This same mistake is being made continually by people who are accustomed to the conditions prevalent in a level country with a practically uniform temperature and an atmosphere having high relative humidity. They have no knowledge of the effect of altitude differences, have only the haziest of notions about irrigation and dry farming, and no conception of the effect a dry atmosphere has upon temperature variations. They know very well the difference between the numerous varities of apples and would consider locality, soil, etc., very carefully before selecting the varities to be planted in a given region, but a cactus is a cactus only, to them, and they assume that one kind ought to do what any other will.

Another disappointment which had to be met was that even cacti must have some water in order to grow. It isn't very much, as compared with the requirements of most other plants, but it is some, and up to the maximum limit (which is considerable) the more water they get the more they grow, other things being equal. Then, too, a crop of cactus is not as valuable forage as a crop of alfalfa. The attitude of mind of the average man seems to be that because it isn't, therefore, the cactus is as he used to think it—good for nothing. It is in order to point out a few of the uses and their very definite limitations that this bulletin is written.

AS A STOCK FOOD.

Cacti have been used as a stock food for a long time and for several kinds of stock, hence there is nothing radically new in the process. The new part is that Americans generally have just recently found it out, probably most largely by the work of Mr. Luther Burbank. Various genera and species have been used, mostly the spiny one, hence the spineless species are not a necessity for this purpose. While other kinds have been and can be used, the species of Opuntia are by far the most important for this purpose, and the flat-jointed species known to Americans as "prickly pears," and to the Mexicans as "nopales," are those which are and will continue to be the kinds utilized. The reason for this is purely that of the abundance of material in this group. Men always use first what come most readily to their hands, and the flat-jointed Opuntias are more abundant as species and as individuals than are the species of any other genus in the family. Next in importance are certain species of the Cylindropuntias, but these can never be more than of very secondary importance because they reproduce themselves so much more slowly, either naturally or artificially, than do prickly pears.   The latter grow from cuttings with the utmost ease if the cuttings are properly calloused before planting.

This process should receive special mention because it is a practice so at variance with ordinary procedure in the handling of plants.   Cactus joints which are to be planted should be allowed to lie in the sunlight in a dry place until the cut

surfaces have thoroughly calloused, before they are put into
the ground. This may take a week or more, depending upon the
dryness of the air. If the cuttings are not treated in this way a
very large proportion of them will rot, especially if the soil in
which they are planted be wet—as it should be to produce the best
rooting.

The uses of the prickly pear (as well as the limitations of
these uses) as forage plants have been exhaustively discussed
by Dr. Griffiths and Prof. Hare in bulletins* available to the public that very little need be said here. Bulletin No. 74 referred to
is particularly complete and concise in its statements on the subject, but we wish to elaborate a few of these "heads" with especial
reference to conditions that prevail in New Mexico.

The first point which must be emphasized is that even cacti
must have *some* water in order to live and grow, and that the
learger the amount of water available (up to the maximum that
they can use, and other things being equal) the greater the
amount of forage or fruit will a given kind produce on a given
area.

As has already been pointed out, the mesas of the southern
and lower parts of the state which have a moderately high winter
temperature receive so little water that even the hardiest of the
native species grow but slowly. There is no doubt that larger
crops of cacti could be obtained from these mesas if there were
more water, and the only way more water can be obtained is by some
sort of irrigation system. If an irrigation system were installed,
the cost of installation and operation would necessitate the cultivation of some more valuable crop. There is no doubt that immense
crops of certain kinds of cacti could be grown in the valley soils
of the southern part of the state, but those same soils will produce
much more valuable crops of something else, so they are not used
for cacti. Certain parts of the state receive enough rainfall to produce a good crop of cacti, but these localities are so cold in both
winter and summer that none but the hardiest species will grow
there.

*The value of the cactus as an economic plant lies in its ability
to utilize most effectively a scanty and very irregular water supply.*

Another idea which needs to be very plainly expressed is that

---

*Bull. 74, 102, Bureau of Plant Industry and Bull. 91, Bureau of Animal Industry,
Washington, D. C. Bull. 60, 69, N. M. Exp. Station, Agricultural College.

cactus will never supplant alfalfa as a forage plant, nor will it even be a competitor. Nor is it an ideal forage plant under the best of conditions. It has some very serious drawbacks, but it also has some good qualities, the most pronounced of which is that it will thrive where most other plants die. Within their limitations the cacti are good for a certain restricted number of uses.

On the stock ranges of New Mexico today are large quantities of prickly pear which have a value as forage, and this crop is especially valuable in the times of drought which visit all parts of the state at more or less irregular intervals. This forage, while it is not as good as grama grass, is much better than nothing, and in dry years the feed is reduced to cactus or nothing. In the past it has been the custom of stockmen to take the "nothing" and let the cactus remain where it is. There have been two or three aparently sufficient reasons for this, as follows: 1st, The cattle are not accustomed to eat the cacti and would have to be taught to use it. 2nd, When they are forced to take to a cactus diet they are weak and the scouring due to the large quantities of inorganic salts taken with this kind of food is said to still further weaken them, thus increasing the loss. 3rd, There is some work and expense connected with the preparation of the cacti for use by the stock. Since this seems like putting more money into a proposition which is bound to lose anyhow, most of the stockmen sell off what they can get to walk off the range and trust to luck that some of the others will pull through, and pocket their losses.

It seems to the author that a better plan would be to accustom one's stock to eating cactus as part of the ration all the time, thus obviating the first and to some extent the second difficulty. And the work necessary to accustom stock to the practice would also accustom the man to the work and would necessitate the purchase of all needful tools or apparatus. If this were done little by little during a period when forage was normally abundant, the expense and labor would hardly be felt and the stock would gradually acquire the habit and learn to like the feed. Then, when the drought came, there would be little change in the whole procedure except an increase in the amount of cactus fed. A small amount of prickly pear is said to be good for young stock for toning them up, especially if they have been on dry feed for a long time. Thus by a small outlay for tools and a little work, the stockman would be able to turn to good use that which is now considered useless and more or less of a nuisance.

Another procedure, associated with this proposed practice, whicn seems wise to the author, is the planting of certain areas of the range in cactus. Most of the stock ranges have areas of broken land where grass does not grow well or has been killed out and replaced by weeds, where cacti would grow. Such a crop would be very important during seasons of drought. It would also tend to prevent the erosion that is now so rapid in such situations. Some experiments have been carried on by this station on the growing of cacti and the following results have been obtained:

Well calloused cuttings of the flat jointed species root readily at almost any time of the year, but do best in the spring and early summer. We planted joints about one year old, and those about two years old, and some that were several years old. All of them grew, with an average of about 98% rooting. Practically all old woody joints and all rooted joints, no matter how dry they were, grew. Old joints are not only a little more apt to grow well, but they are somewhat less apt to be attacked by rabbits and other small animals that eat the younger more succulent joints and do considerable damage to plants that are just starting, by pulling them loose after they have commenced to root.

Of 100 joints that were simply thrown flat on the ground and stepped on (to force the spines down and bring the joints in contact with the soil) 85 rooted and grew, but they were about one year longer in reaching a given stage of development than joints planted (i. e. put part way in the ground and the earth "firmed" around them) at the same time. For cheapness this method of planting an area would be much the best, if there were no particular hurry as to when a crop should be forthcoming.

As an inexpensive reserve supply of food stored against a season of drought, there is nothing now known which can compete with cactus in the arid Southwest, since it slowly accumulates during the favorable seasons and is ready to be called upon when the unfavorable one comes.

The cacti are favorable from another standpoint. They do best in locations which are not as suitable for the grasses, seeming to prefer rocky and broken ground to the flatter areas with compact soils, hence the two could be handled together on most of the ranges of the state and would tend to supplement each other.

Another advantage associated with the feeding of cactus comes from the succulent character of the feed. Stock must eat a large amount, when it is used as the only roughage, in order to get sufficient solids, and since the joints contain a large percentage of water, the animals drink less water when on this feed. This is a decided advantage at any time to stock, stockman, and range. It reduces the amount of walking necessary for the first, makes the water supply of the range go farther, and cuts the range up less, all of which are advantageous to the stockman.

With the suggestion that cacti be planted, the question at once arises as to what kind to plant. There is nothing better yet known for New Mexico conditions than the species native in the locality where it may be desirable to plant. In the northern part of the state there are two common species either of which will grow. These are *Opuntia phaeacantha** and *O. polyacantha.* The former is the more desirable, as it is of good size and a free grower, but it requires considerable moisture and there are many places where it will not grow. In such places *O. polyacantha* will do well. In the southern part of the state wherever there is enough moisture *O. engelmanni* is doubtless the best thing to grow on account of its size, though many of the other species would be much better than nothing and should be utilized wherever it is possible. The general rule to be followed is to plant that species which is best adapted to the conditions prevalent in the region and which grows most rapidly and produces the most forage in a given time.

Stated in a few words the author believes that, by proper management, it is possible to have these plants store up forage during the favorable years, that may be utilized in the years of drought, if stockmen will but encourage the spread of the plant in situations where nothing else grows and teach their animals to like this kind of food. He appreciates the fact that he has had no actual experience, but there is plenty of evidence that it can be done, since it has often been done by different people and in different ways.

The argument in favor of using native species is very strongly emphasized by our experience in trying to grow two species as field crops upon the mesa without irrigation. In the experiment two

---

*See discussion of species further on.

species were chosen that were growing more or less abundantly in the immediate region. One of them (*Opuntia engelmanni*) grows well in the foot-hills of the mountains and among rocks at an elevation of 4,500 to 5,500 feet, where the rainfall is probably about 12 inches* and where it makes plants 3 to 4 feet tall and has large joints. The other species (*O. dulcis*)† is one which has been introduced into the Mesilla Valley from farther south. In the heavier valley soils it grows without any attention or extra water. We had grown both species on the mesa in small quantities for several years without protection of any kind and with only a little additional water above what fell. (The records of the nearby rain-gauge show an average annual precipitation at this point of about 9 inches).

In a number of ways *O. dulcis* promised most. Its joints were more succulent and less spiny; it grew more rapidly than the other species; it produced more fruit and the fruit was sweeter and had smaller seeds and a thinner rind. The idea that it was not as hardy was in no way indicated by its growth in the valley. Both species were put in a poorer, more sandy, and drier soil, so the chances looked to be about equal for each.

The distance to the mountains is a number of miles, hence the transportation of the cuttings of *O. engelmanni* was a laborious and expensive proposition. The result was that the cuttings planted were of single joints and of all ages. The material of *O. dulcis* was abundant and most of the cuttings planted were of three joints and a good many of them already rooted.

The first season after the planting was particularly favorable in the matter of rainfall, and the *O. dulcis* plants, having already stored moisture, grew vigorously and the experiment looked very successful. Very few of the *O. engelmanni* cuttings produced a single new joint that season, while many of the larger *O. dulcis* plants more than doubled their size. The following winter was dry, so dry that all available food for the wild animals of the region was exhausted and the only succulent food remaining was the cactus of which the experiment station patch was in the best condition and very conveniently located. The result was that the rabbits almost ate up the plants of the *O. dulcis* that winter and spring. We had depended upon the spines of both species to pro-

---

*No accurate data are to be had, hence this is an estimate.
†Referred to in previous bulletins of this station as *O. laevis?*

tect them from animals but the young joints were not sufficiently spiny to perform this duty for the *O. dulcis* plants. The others were hardly touched. We put out poison and killed some of the rabbits but didn't save the plants. The next season we fenced the patch with a fine meshed wire fence and covered the bottom of the fence with dirt, but it was necessary to watch it all the time and stop runways burrowed under the wire.

We have replanted the field as far as necessary twice since the first planting, but the precipitation has been very scanty for the past four seasons and the plants have grown very little.

In the spring of 1909 just after the plants had begun to grow there was a pretty heavy frost and all the young joints on the *O. dulcis* plants were frozen, though plants of the same species less than a quarter of a mile away at a slightly lower level were barely touched. The patch of a little over two acres of the *O. dulcis* now, five years after planting, has less cactus on it than it had at the end of the first growing season. And this is a moderately spiny species that is seemingly well able to take care of itself less than half a mile away and only a few feet lower than where we tried it. The experiment demonstrates that *O. dulcis* needs a slightly warmer locality, a more compact soil, (though this is of less importance), and more water than it can get on the mesas near the Agricultural College.

The *O. engelmanni* plants have grown very slowly but have mostly survived the adverse conditions of the new environment. They have suffered none from cold and little from rabbits because they are spiny and tough. How much of them the rabbits would have eaten if the more desirable *O. dulcis* had not been nearby cannot even be estimated. But they have suffered for lack of water all the time and at the end of five years are hardly larger than they ought to be at the end of the second growing season. It is probable that any one of the three species which grow naturally upon this mesa would have produced several times the amount of forage on the same area with less care and expense, but the experimenter didn't think them worth the trial and even cut some of them out of the patch when planting the species selected. It is also likely that these species could have protecetd themselve better from the rabbits, since they maintain a continued existence in the region where the rabbits abound.

Not one of the known spineless species would endure any of the three adverse conditions of this situation, and the locality chosen is one of the warmest places in the state, receives about the average rainfall for the lower levels of the southern part and has about the average supply of cactus-eating rodents.

As an experiment giving data as to rate of production of fodder per acre it has been a complete failure, or rather has shown that the attempt to grow these species at that place as forage plants is utterly useles. It has most effectively demonstrated the importance of spines to these plants.

Another small planting (2,000 cuttings of each of two varieties) was made in an inclosed area in the foot-hills of the Organ mountains. The species chosen were *Opuntia engelmanni* and *Opuntia arborescens,* both of which were already growing on the land. The region is very rocky and the soil quite scanty, hence it was to be expected that the number of cuttings rooting would be much less than occurred in the mesa soils of the cactus garden, but the result was a surprise to us. Of the 2,000 cuttings of the cane cactus planted only 5 grew, while only about 40% of the other species grew. These results were partly due to the rabbits, since the fence was only designed to keep cattle out and did not protect from small animals. But both species are very spiny and grow in the region all the time. In making the plantings we planted 1,000 young joint cuttings and 1,000 second year or older cuttings of each species, to find out about the relative rate of rooting in these different cuttings. This placed tender succulant joints with poorly developed armature on the ground where the rabbits could get at them and they "did the rest." They ate many of the joints almost completely and pulled many more of them up. (It can hardly be said they pulled them out of the soil, for the small angular rock fragments of the area were much more abundant than soil, but the location was the most favorable of the region and hundreds of tons of one of the species used were growing within a stone's throw of where the cuttings were planted.)

These experiments demonstrate the delicate adjustment between plants and their environment and emphasize once more the extreme slowness of plant reproduction and growth under desert conditions. The stubby, dwarfed vegetation of arid lands spell in years what the forests do in the humid regions—i. e. the ultimate output of the region, the factor of time having been entirely neglected, since there has been plently of time. The only thing lacking has been water and that is and will continue to be lacking.

There has been but little done in the way of investigating the use of cactus by sheep and goats but it seems to the author that there is a possibility here needing investigation. Goats will nibble at the spiny species as we have observed on one or two occasions, and would probably eat the singed plants freely. And there is reason to believe that sheep would do the same thing. The low species common in the northern part of the state where sheep are most extensively raised would seem to be particularly promising for this purpose. .

Another use suggested by Mr. C. B. Allaire, of San Antonio, New Mexico, is that of a part of the ration for ewes while lambing. One difficulty experienced by sheepmen is that of finding a supply of succulent feed for the ewes at the lambing time. We are told that if they do not have enough of such feed their milk becomes scanty and very rich which is bad for the lambs and, in consequence, a large percentage of the latter die. The difficulty is one which arises from the necessity of holding the herd in one place for a long time, and the consequent disappearance of the green feed. All the conditions tend to dry up the ewes' milk, resulting in constipation in the lambs. A partial ration of cactus at this time should be beneficial in several ways. It would prevent such close grazing of the more succulent forage; make it possible for the ewes to use even more of the browse of the region; reduce the amount of water necessary for the band; furnish a laxative for the ewes and probably through the milk to the lambs; furnish the necessary succulent feed and thus prevent the drying up of the ewe's milk and so prevent the loss of the lambs. The experiment seems to be well worth trying; especially would it seem to be worth while in those years when there is little spring precipitation and no succulent feed for the ewes at lambing time—a condition which arises all too frequently in New Mexico. What has been said of sheep would probably apply to goats as well, though we have not heard such losses reported for that kind of stock.

Other factors of economic importance in the use of cacti as stock feed, that has been discussed at length by Dr. Griffiths and Prof. Hare, concern the methods of preparing the feed for the stock. To summarize these, it may be said that the joints may be cut by power driven choppers; or the spines may be singed by holding joints in the flames of a brush fire on a pitchfork; or they may be singed with a "pear burner"—a gasoline torch something like a plumber's torch but adapted to the purpose. The last method is most satisfactory in the pasture, since the work of gathering the crop is then done by the animals. For feeding to dairy cattle in the barns or for feeding beef cattle in pens, the choppers are extensively used in certain localities where the feed is abundant and does not have to be hauled a great distance. That cactus joints contain relatively large quantities of inorganic salts which act as purgatives has been shown by the chemical analysis of the joints. The fact that cactus fed animals scour was already well known, but feeding experiments for both milk and beef production have show no deleterious effect to the animals experimented with, and they have maintained or gained weight and maintained the quantity and·quality of milk produced, while appearing to be in as good or better health than the remainder of the herd. Experience has shown that cattle fed on singed or chopped cactus suffer little or none from the spines.

FOR MILCH COWS.

Another use of cacti, which is of particular importance in New Mexico, is as a part of the ration for milch cows, especially for dairy stock. No very satisfactory pasture grass for this purpose has yet been discovered in our state and the result is that most milch cows are fed on dry feed the year around, and many of them never go out of the corral. For such stock a cactus patch offers a much needed succulent feed and equally needed exercise in gathering it. Dairymen in Texas have been using such cactus pastures with excellent results for a number of years.* The cactus is to be fed as part of the ration only and part of it should be fed chopped and mixed with the grain feed at the regular feeding time. Where cottonseed meal is used the ration of meal should be sprinkled over the chopped cactus and the two fed together. Other ground feeds could be fed in the same way. In the feeding experiments referred to in the bulletin mentioned it was demonstrated that chopped cactus could be used as part or all the roughage in the ration without loss in quantity of the milk produced and that the cows enjoyed the feed.

---

*See Bull. No. 91, Bureau of Animal Industry, U. S. Dept. Ag.

There is probably not a farm or a dairy in this state on which a small area of land could not be profitably used as a cactus patch for the milch cows. If this were properly chosen it need not be valuable land, since the cacti will grow on land too rough for ordinary farming operations. The only requirement would be that it be so situated as to be not too wet at any time and yet get enough water to supply the small demands of the species grown. If the area were fenced and not close to the mesa where rabbits would be abundant, the more nearly spineless the cactus grown the better. But any kind of prickly pear would be better than none, though the spinier kinds are more unpleasant to handle and harder for the stock to eat.

The argument in favor of this procedure is particularly applicable to dairymen who must furnish and handle large quantities of feed for their cows all the time. Such men always have land that could be used for this purpose and which is not in use otherwise; the native prickly pear of his own region is to be had for the planting and will cost only the work of getting it; the planting may be of the simplest kind if, he chooses to wait for the growth of the plants, i. e. merely scattering the joints on the ground; by using power driven chopping machines the feed may be prepared for use and the workmen handle it all the time with forks or shovels; by using the "pear burners" the standing plants may be singed in the pasture, just enough for the day's feed, and the cows left to gather it.

The spinier species of cactus singe as readily if not more so than those with fewer spines, and they are much better able to take care of themselves while the spines are on. Cattle accustomed to eating singed cactus will follow the burner in the patch or will come to the brush fire where it is singed, when this is the method used.

Once more we wish to emphasize that fact that the great value of this plant as source of succulent feed as well as for roughage lies in is ability to take up water whenever it can get it and utilize nearly all of it for making forage.

Exeperience has shown that cattle prefer the older joints to the young, leathery ones; that they will eat frozen ones; that they learn to enjoy the feed; that the spines of chopped cactus bother them very little when fed with other roughage; that after they learn to eat the cactus they will work on the spiny unsinged plants, thus demonstrating that the spines bother them very little. Another advantage of this feed as a succulent portion of a ration is that it is at its very best for feeding purposes in the winter time when other succulent feed is scarce or entirely lacking.

THORNLESS CACTUS.

There is no doubt that species of several of the genera of the cactus family will warrant this title and that many are well known to be thornless and spineless. Most of these are not meant, however, when that expression is used and are not to be considered here. But by "thornless cactus" or "spineless cactus" is meant those "prickly pears" without or with but few of the larger spines or thorns and with a reduced number of the smaller spines or spicules that are usually so common on the joints of these plants. Dr. Griffiths has fully discussed this question in a bulletin entitled "The 'Spineless' Prickly Pears," and has stated very clearly the value of these plants and their very evident limitations in a number of ways.

The general impression has been given out, by various publications in the nature of advertising matter, that these spineless forms are recent "creations" of the horticulturist and that they are some of the most wonderful of "finds." There is certainly not the least doubt that the "spineless" or "thornless' kinds have been in cultivation in Mexico since before the time of Columbus, and that practically smooth species have been in cultivation in the Mediteranean region for a number of generations. The origin of these spineless varieties is shrouded in uncertainty just as are the origins of many of our garden vegetables and cultivated fruit and field crops.

The next important statement is that these plants are restricted in two very important ways in their distribution . They were supposed to be absolutely independent of a water supply and their relation to temperature · extremes was not properly considered when the advertising matter was printed.

The experience of the writer (already published in an annual report of this station) may be reported here. He believed the statements with regard to their resistance. Through the kindness of the Division of Plant Introduction, Bureau of Plant Industry, Washington, he received eight specimens of the spineless forms from the Mediterranean region, and 100 seedlings of spineless parentage from California. Six of the eight European specimens (which were almost perfectly smooth) grew well in the cactus garden during the summer. The other two had been bruised in shipment and never rooted. Ninety-seven out of the 100 seedlings grew very well, though all of them were quite spiny. We were much elated over our success (?) and were expecting much of these plants, all of them being very vigorous growers. However, nothing was done to protect them during the winter and they all froze early, though the season was in no way different from what was to be expected every winter.

The next spring we told our experience to the company then offering spineless varieties for sale in California, and agreed to buy cuttings of all varieties which they offered as being able to stand the winter temperatures of southern New Mexico. We received a very courteous letter in which we were informed that a variety which had the desired characteristics had not yet been produced but that experiments looking in that direction were in progress. Since that time we have had in cultivation some of the hardiest of the spineless varities, growing them in the open in the summer and in the greenhouse in the winter, but the conditions are not favorable for them and they have grown slowly and none of them have bloomed.

One season we were supplied with a few flowers of spineless varieties when our native specimens were in bloom and over 100 pollinations of the native species were made with pollen from these flowers. Although all possible care was taken in these experiments, none of the flowers so treated set fruit. We have since learned that it has been the experience of others who have attempted to do breeding, that the cross from stamens of spineless to pistils of spiny varieties has rarely produced fruit. It thus becomes evident at once that southern New Mexico is hardly an ideal place for this breeding work, and southern New Mexico is more favorable than other parts of the state. Nevertheless, we have a number of spineless species growing in the greenhouse and hope to try some of this work whenever these plants bloom. It will be necessary to do this breeding work under glass because the plants in the greenhouse commence to grow in the spring before those out of doors and before the former dare be put outside. We have so far been unable to retard their growth at this period though we may succeed. We have native species in cultivation with them which will no doubt bloom earlier inside and from which pollen may be obtained.

We have been endeavoring to get growing plants of all the New Mexican species in our cactus garden with the idea of studying all of them in the search for those having particular qualities that may be turned to account in any way. Among those which promise most is a species found four or five years ago in the Sacramento Mountains near Alamogordo by Mr. A. B. Dille and named for him by Dr. Griffiths. Through the kindness of Mr. Dille we were furnished with a number of cuttings of this species and now have the plant growing in the garden. In cultivation it is more spiny than the original description calls for, but it is a fairly free grower with large joints bearing few spines and spicules, and is hardy to the winter temperatures of southern New Mexico. Whether it will grow in the northern and colder parts of the state remains to be seen. It will need more water than is afforded by the mesas of the southern part of the state.

To summarize the present status of the "thornless cactus" in New Mexico we may say: None of the highly advertised species so far offered will endure our winter temperatures; the European and Mexican species are subject to the same restrictions; none of them will be able to get along on the water supply of the open mesas of southern New Mexico, through occasional sags or basin-like depressions, where flood waters irrigate the ground at irregular intervals, would receive enough water to make them grow. There is a single native "near spineless" species which promises to live in such sags or basins; spineless cactus of any kind will never endure on the open ranges,—they must always be protected from stock in some way or other.

Our experience with the cultivation of a very spiny and a moderately spiny species amply demonstrates the futility of trying to grow a crop of spineless *Opuntias* on the open range. The cuttings would be eaten before they could take root. This reduces the spineless cactus to a field crop at the outset, and as a field crop its usefulness is limited to very definite purposes and particular treatments. The spiny species are those which may be of value as range plants.

FOR HUMAN FOOD.

For a detailed discussion of the possible uses of the fruit of the

PLATYOPUNTIAE—the *tuna* of the Mexican or "prickly pear" of the American—the reader is referred to bulletin number 64 of this station and bulletin number 116 of the Bureau of Plant Industry, U. S. Department of Agriculture, Washington. These bulletins, prepared by Dr. David Griffiths and Prof. R. F. Hare, treat the subject most exhaustively from the economic, the botanical and the chemical sides. Since few if any of the species of Opuntia producing commercially valuable *tunas* will grow in New Mexico, and other uses similar to those now in common practice in Mexico have not yet been established in this state, there is little need to say much about this phase of the subject and nothing more than a synopsis of the work of the gentlemen mentioned above will be given.

To speak of a tuna is like speaking of an apple or peach or any other cultivated fruit; there are many well recognized kinds, each with its own good qualities. These different kinds having been produced by natural selection are usually recognized as species by systematists, though our cultivated fruits, having been produced by artificial selection are referred to as varieties. As with apples, tunas are good in different ways and in different degrees, and the users have their preferences among the different kinds.

Fresh tunas are eaten, during the season of ripe fruit, in large quantities by the poorer class of people in parts of Mexico as a regular article of diet, and they form a large and important part of the ration with many. The number of tunas eaten per day is seemingly very large, but it must be remembered that the pulpy portion actually of food value is very much like the pulp of a watermelon and must be taken in large amounts to supply any large quantity of solid food, because by far the greater portion of it is water. Besides this use as a staple article of diet, which is, of course, the most important use of the fresh fruit, they are used by many as merely a refreshing portion of the meal, as one eats any kind of fruit, and are enjoyed in this way by many.

None of the wild species of tuna that grow in New Mexico are particularly palatable though most of them may be eaten without any deleterious effect. But they are usually small with a thick rind and many spines and seeds, so there is not much of the fruit which is really edible and that little is hard to get and insipid as well. Most Americans who try to eat the fruit make the mistake of eating the rind which is often, in fact usually, as large a

proportion of the fruit as is the seed containing pulp. It would
be as sensible to condemn watermelon as of no value because one
cannot eat the rind. Another feature in the case is one of personal taste. Most people have to acquire a liking for many of the
fruits that they ultimately learn to enjoy very much. The writer's
experience has been that he had to learn to eat bananas and has
so far failed to like tomatoes though they "look good." He did
not like the taste of tunas at first but has gotten so he will eat
the native New Mexican fruit much as boys eat wild gooseberries
and ground cherries, and rather enjoys them. He would soon
acquire a taste for the cultivated kind.

Besides the fresh fruit many manufactured products are prepared from them and offered in the markets of Mexico, whence
they go to be used as food by the people. *Miel de Tuna* (pronounced
Mee-ell day too-nah) is a syrup about the consistency of
honey or molasses made by boiling down the crushed pulp of the
fruits and then straining out the seeds. After further boiling
and a special kind of stirring while it cools, the product is complete. It gradually candies, but, if properly prepared will keep
indefinitely without souring. *Melcocha* (Mell-co-chah) and *queso
de tuna* (Kay-so day too-nah) are solid products of about the consistency of ordinary cheese that are made by evaporating the juice
of seeded and crushed fruit to a certain degree of dryness and
kneading or stirring the product while cooling. The sugar in the
melcocha begins to crystalize in a month or so and ultimately the
whole product "candies" as in the case of *miel de tuna*. The
treatment given the *queso* is such as to prevent the crystalization
of the sugar and the only effect of age on the product is to harden
it by drying. In the better prepared product it is customary to
wrap the small cubes in tin foil which protects the *queso* from
dirt and evaporation. *Colonche* (Ko-lone-chay) is a fermented
drink made from these fruits. The pulp, with seeds included, is
boiled slowly for two or three hours and then strained, the liquid
being set away to cool and ferment. It is used for about twenty
days after fermentation begins, getting more strongly intoxicating
as it ages.

FOR DECORATIVE PURPOSES.

Because of their very bizarre appearance and their strikingly
handsome flowers, taken with the ease of transportation and pro-
pagation, the cacti have been for a long time in cultivation, and

a considerable industry has been established in Europe in producing these plants for those interested in growing them. A few collectors in the arid regions of our own country and Mexico are kept busy supplying the demand for our native species and this demand is gradually increasing as more people learn of the beauties of these very peculiar plants.

They are particularly well adapted to conditions in New Mexico, because they need relatively little water to live and it makes very little difference to them when the water comes, and they are always prepared for a long drought. If kept dry, the native species can nearly all endure low temperatures and there is little doubt that many species restricted in distribution and not now found here will grow very well. A case in point is that of *Opuntia basilaris* Engelman, which grows excellently in southern New Mexico, though native in southern Utah and Nevada. It is one of the best of Opuntias for decorative purposes as it has reddish joints, no spines though numerous spicules, and large, rose-purple or almost crimson flowers. It is a free bloomer and perfectly hardy. Several of the Arizona species are valuable additions to any collection and will, no doubt, grow in New Mexico.

For outdoor planting they lend themselves to formal gardening and work into rockeries most excellently. They may be massed in beds of different shape, heed being taken of the habits of growth of the different species used. By proper selection and arrangement it is possible to have some plants in flower most of the season, since the native species bloom at different times from early in April until the first of August, and some of them have bright colored fruits on them all through the winter, the fruit appearing long after the flowers are gone. Certain species have brightly colored conspicuous spines that add to the beauty of the plants.

For our region these plants are particularly valuable (as are many of the native plants) because they are adapted to the variable temperatures, the intense light, and the long periods of drought. Adapted as they are to a small supply of water they do well when put under cultivation, and when given a little extra water they respond by growing vigorously and flowering profusely. And if for any one of the dozen of common reasons, the irrigation system ceases to furnish the usual supply of water—as they all do sooner or later—these plants do not die as other will and always do. They simply suspend active operations and draw on their supply of stored moisture for that necessary for life. They do not grow, but they do not die as most other plants do under such conditions. They may even bloom if the blooming season has arrived. In the cultivation of cacti there are several points that should be kept in mind. Most of our native species grow best if the specimen planted has a root. The roots may have been much cut up and dried out, but when placed in the ground and wet they soon send out new branches.

Species of *Echinocereus, Echinocactus,* and *Mamillaria* will hardly grow from cuttings that are not rooted. The flat jointed Opuntias grow well from such cuttings if properly rooted, but even they do best when rooted joints are planted. The results obtained by various methods of planting joints of the PLATYOPUNTIAE have already been discussed and so need not be repeated, but the best usage is to plant old, calloused cuttings. CYLINDROPUNTIAE do not grow well from cuttings, and we have never tried to propagate any of the other kinds in this way, since the rooted specimens were as easily obtained as a cutting would be. The CYLINDROPUNTIAE probably reproduce rather freely from seeds, as young plants of *O. arborescens* are common on the mesas and they are usually in clusters of small rooted plants sprouting from near the same point (probably a fruit having been covered, several of the seeds have germinated together sending up a cluster of seedlings). Many of the *Echinocerei* and *Mamillariae* branch freely from the base and ultimately develop roots on these lateral branches. Such groups may be divided and will develop new root systems and form other clusters.

Several of our species prefer a limestone soil and will not live long if grown in a soil without a considerable amount of lime salts present. *Echinocereus chloranthus, E. dasyacanthus, E. stramineus, Echinocactus horizonthalonius, Mamillaria micromeris, M. lasiacantha, M. tuberculosa, and M. grahami* have all shown a marked preference for a limestone soil and there are doubtless others that prefer it. We have succeeded in growing these species once by building a mound of the common mesa soil over a wagon load or two of broken up limestone, and another time by mixing some old plaster into the soil. Aside from this demand made by some species for abundant limestone in the soil, the only other require-

ment made by the plants is that the soil shall be open and porous
and well drained. None of them will endure a cold, wet, compact
soil. Plants may be transplanted at practically any time in the
year, though they do a little better if transplanted in the winter
or spring.

Normally it is the temperature which causes these plants tc
commence growing and when it warms up to the proper degree
they usually commence to grow whether there has been any precipitation or not. If such plants have been rendered succulent and
thick by an extra supply of water and are then subjected to freezing temperature they are much more apt to be killed. The writer
was told that New Mexico species of cacti grew and endured the
winters of Washington, D. C. very well so long as they were kept
dry and not allowed to freeze after growth had commenced in
the spring.

One danger in the artificial cultivation of these plants is of
getting them too wet.   Plants supplied with too much water
become very succulent and are ultimately attacked by some sort
of mould, and rot very rapidly and completely. Care should be
taken not to bruise the plants since this generally results in the
rotting. In greenhouse cultivation it is necessary to establish good
drainage in all the pots and beds and be careful to sprinkle only
when the sun is shining. These two precautions prevent a large
part of the rotting that would otherwise occur. In laying out
beds it is quite effective to mass plants of the same species rather
than to plant the individuals separately and scattered. This last
method is the natural one and the only one that can be success-
fully followed if the plants are to shift for themselves. If massed
close together they must be given additional water and the soil
must be fertilized, since the unfertilized soils and the unaided
rainfall are only sufficient to suport a scattered vegetation such
as covers the mesas naturally. If either of these requirements is
ignored the plants will gradually die out until they are as far
apart as will result in the density of plant life that the soil and
water supply will support. Of course, the fertilization need come
only at long intervals and the additional water can come at almost
any convenient time, though preferably it should come in the
early summer when the plants are growing most rapidly.

Another advantage cacti have over most other plants is the
ease with which old and large plants may be transplanted. It is

possible to transplant plants of any age and at almost any time if they are carefully handled so as to avoid bruising and if the root system is maintained and water supplied immediately. This enables one to have his flower bed as he wants it without waiting years for it to grow.

OPUNTIA.

This is by far the largest genus of cacti and New Mexico has about as many species as of all others put together. It is the most varied in appearance also, having three or four well differentiated types that at first sight or in their more highly specialized forms do not seem to be very closely related. Economically this is much the most important genus as well, since many of the species are valuable from the forage they produce, and their fruits also are of value. The flat jointed species (PLATYOPUNTIAE) or "prickly pears" are known almost everywhere in the United States, especially since the recent advertising of the spineless or thornless cacti cultivated in southern California and adjacent regions. The economic possibilities of these plants have already been discussed in considerable detail in this bulletin. They also have their possible uses as decorative plants which are appreciated by but few people—the so-called fanciers—who are really those individuals who have in one way or another become interested in them and have become fascinated with their great complexity and peculiar beauties. Attention should be called to a comon mistake in connection with the "prickly pear" The large circular or elongated, flat, green parts of which the plants are composed are not 'leaves" in the sense that we use the term when speaking of the leaves of a tree, but are subdivisions or joints of a peculiarly constructed flattened and jointed stem. They function as leaves as do the thickened stems of all the species in the family (with an exception or two).

The various species all agree in having rudimentary leaves that are thick, fleshy outgrowths generally ¼ of an inch long or less, round and tapering to a point, appearing on the areolae of the young joints and bases of the flowers and falling off before the joints are mature or as soon as the flower blooms. The spines are of two kinds, one set of stout spines from the center of the areolae, of various sizes, colors and numbers, and a set of small ones variously called spicules, glochids, or setae by different writers. All the spines and spicules are barbed backward so that these organs penetrate very readily but come out very reluctantly and cause pain to one who is impaled. The spicules are particularly troublesome since they break away from the plant very easily, and many of them are so small as to be seen with difficulty though one be acutely conscious of their presence.   The fruits of this genus are nearly always covered with areolae bearing spicules, but without proper spines. The joints are of various shapes; the fruits are of different sizes, dry or succulent, tuberculate or smooth, of various colors, purple, red, greenish, and various shapes from spheroidal to long cylindric or club-shaped. The seeds are mostly large and light colored, somewhat unevenly discoid, or variously angled, and surrounded by a more or less prominent thickened ridge about the center (edge) of the disk.

With the exception of three of the CYLINDROPUNTIAE, all of the species of *Opuntia* here listed have yellow flowers of much the same general shape, differing in the shade of yellow and in size, to some degree. The base of the flower is short and thick, sometimes nearly spherical, again elongated and tapering at the base. The tube formed by the united bases of the petals is very short and the petals usually open in the shape of a rounded cup. The petals change in color with the age of the flower, usually they are lighter when they open than at any other time, generally a pale lemon yellow, and change to an orange color that afternoon. In most of the species the petals close during the first night and on the second day when they open they are always darker colored, in some cases becoming almost a reddish brown, at least at the bases of the petals. Most of the flowers open for two successive days only, and then only in bright sunlight. The three species mentioned as exceptions have purple flowers, two of them bright bluish purple, the other a dull, faded purple streaked with green.

Our native species will be most easily understood if considered in sub-groups, containing forms actually different but closely resembling each other. The common flat jointed "prickly pears" having flattened, disk-like or oval joints constitute the large group well known to everyone. For convenience we have to consider these in sub-divisions, those with dry fruit and those with pulpy fruit and of the latter some are erect or nearly so and the remainder are nearly prostrate upon the ground. Another group of species more or less well known is the CYLINDROPUNTIAE with round stems of various diameters from ¼ of an inch to one inch; most of these have dry, tuberculate fruit, one having a small, pulpy, scarlet berry. The other two groups, the CLAVATAE (referring to the club-shaped joints) and the TUMIDAE (referring to the swelled or distended condition of the joints), have very few representatives in the state and are known to only a few people. In the former the joints are round but taper from the base to the top, thus giving the appearance of a somewhat swelled club. This group contains 3 species. The other group, with 2 or possibly 3 species, consists of plants with very small joints that when dry resemble some of the flat jointed species but when supplied with plenty of water they become distended and about half rounded. These are the TUMIDAE (meaning "swelled ones"), and they seem to be most nearly related to the *polyacantha* group of the PLAYTOPUNTIAE.

Of the TUMIDAE the two species here listed are easily recognized and are rather widely separated in their distribution. One of them, *Opuntia arenaria* (named *arenaria* because it grows in the sand), was originally described from material collected on sand hills near El Paso and has been found again in the Mesilla Valley just south of Las Cruces. It will probably be found in a number of places up and down the Rio Grande Valley. Its joints are from 1 to 2½ inches long and half as wide, and when growing well, nearly as thick as they are wide. When dry they lose in thickness and become somewhat flattened. They are thickly covered with fine, white spines and have yellow flowers about 1½ inches in diameter. The little plants form low spreading clusters a foot or two in diameter and 6 or 8 inches high and bloom very profusely under favorable conditions. The other species here included in this group is *O. brachyarthra* ("short jointed") originally collected near Inscription Rock in the western part of the state. This little plant has never been collected from the original locality since it was first found and we are not certain that it is specifically distinct from a more northerly species which it closely resembles. It is included here because its type locality is in New Mexico and the name had better stand until we know that it is not distinct from the more northern *O. fragilis* ("fragile") which comes into the mountains of the northern part of the state. Both species (if they are two) have nearly circular joints about 1 inch in diameter that are often swelled up until they are almost as thick. These joints are covered pretty thickly with spines almost as long as the joints; the spines vary in color from white to yellowish brown and from ¾ of an inch to 1 inch long, the lighter, shorter and slenderer ones being common in *O. fragilis* which also has white, woolly areolae. The flowers of both are yellow and from 1 to 2 inches broad. The plants of this group promise little from an economic standpoint, but they are interesting additions to the cactus garden, as showing some more forms that this infinitely variable family of plants can assume.

The three species of the CLAVATAE are not closely alike in general appearance but have three characters in common. Their joints are more or less pronouncedly clavate, i. e. narrow at the bottom and large at the top in the form of an exaggerated club; the stems are more or less tuberculate, the tubercles being merely rounded elevations, not teat-like as in the Mamillaria; and the fruit tubercles are beset with rosette-like clusters of small spines of the same length radiating in a disk from a circular, woolly center. Their differences, which are pronounced, are as follows: *Opuntia emoryi* (Emory's Opuntia, named after Colonel E. H. Emory, who had charge of the first Mexican Boundary Survey) has large, fleshy joints 4 or 5 inches long and 1 to 1½ inches thick with prominent tubercles and large, stout spines, 1½ to 2 inches long, rather light yellowish or pinkish brown and a little flattened. The plants are rarely over two joints high and form irregular beds often 8 or 10 feet across. They grow most readily on sandy mesas and in the arroyos of extreme western New Mexico and adjacent Arizona, being common near Duncan, Arizona on both sides of the line.

Opuntia grahami (Graham's Opuntia) is a small, branching plant forming clumps a foot or so in diameter and 6 or 8 inches high; it grows abundantly on the mesas north and west of El Paso (near which place it was originally collected), and while we have no report of its having been found any place within the limits of this state, it is a very characteristic species which is to be expected on any of the mesas or hills of the southern part of the state. Its joints are slender, rarely over half an inch in diameter, often appearing somewhat shriveled and armed with numerous ashy gray or darker brown and quite round and slender spines that are often 1½ inches long.

Opuntia clavata is the most characteristic species of the group, having strictly clavate or club-shaped joints 2½ to 3½ inches long, and short, white, flattened spines; the main central is usually about 1 inch long, strongly bent downward, flattened and tapering somewhat as a dagger's blade to a sharp point. These little plants spread over the ground also forming beds 6 to 10 feet in diameter, but the plants are scarcely ever over 4 inches high. The beds sometimes are higher than that because of the sand and dirt collected by them.

The CYLINDROPUNTIAE consist of six species in New Mexico which are associated in pairs of closely similar species. They all have cylindrical stems, they are mostly more or less tuberculate, and their fruits are dry and tuberculate (except *O. leptocaulis*). Without exception their spines are covered with loose sheaths, about like thin paper, of various shades. The first pair to be considered are low plants about 1 foot high or less, with stems ½ to ¾ of an inch in diameter and thickly covered with stout, sheathed spines about 1 inch long. The flowers are of medium size, about 2 inches in diameter, and yellow. *Opuntia whipplei* (named in honor of Lt. Whipple in charge of the surveys for a Pacific railroad route near the 35th parallel) has almost white or pale yellow spine sheaths, and form clumps or beds several feet in diameter. It is common along the western edge of the state, north of the middle, and extends into northern Arizona. *Opuntia davisii* (named in honor of Jefferson Davis, the Secretary of War under whom the Pacific railroad surveys were made), is very similar, but its stems are slightly stouter, its spines a little longer and more numerous and the sheaths are a rich golden brown. The only growing plants so far seen by us did not form beds or clumps, but produced single branching plants about 1 foot in diameter in all directions.

The next pair to be considered are *Opuntia leptocaulis* ("slender stemmed") and *O. kleiniae* (in honor of a lady named Klein), both of which (as here considered) are branching shrubs three or four feet high from one or a few central stems. The branches are slender, from ¼ to ½ an inch in diameter, composed of joints of different lengths, some not over an inch long and others a foot or more long; the spines are one (or rarely two) rather long and strongly sheathed spine from each areola. Here the similarity ceases. *O. leptocaulis* has the more slender stems and single (or rarely double) straight spines over an inch long that stand out at right angles to the stems. Its flowers are small (½ to ¾ of an inch) and yellow; its fruit is a bright scarlet berry ¼ to ½ an inch long, succulent, tart, maturing in the winter following the blooming period which is usually in July and August. *O. leptocaulis* (as well as most of the slender stemmed forms) is called *tasajilla* in northern Mexico and this species is often called *"garambullo"* on account of its succulent fruit. The plant here referred to *O. kleiniae* is probably incorrectly named but must go under this name for the time being. It has slightly larger stems, shorter, deflexed, always single spines, its flower is 1½ inches in diameter and of a dull purple with greenish streaks, and its fruit is much larger, ¾ to 1 inch long, somewhat tuberculate, green colored or with reddish tinge and dry at maturity, which occurs the second summer.

The remaining two species of CYLINDROPUNTIAE are large, branching plants that assume a tree-like form when mature. Their smallest (youngest) stems are usually over an inch in diameter, strongly tuberculate, conspicuously spiny.' Both have bright purple flowers 2½ to 3 inches in diameter, followed by tuberculate dry fruit which is green (and sometimes proliferous) until the winter when they become yellow and some of them fall. Of these two species *Opuntia arborescens* (meaning like a small tree) is the commoner throughout the state where it is to be found on the mesas and foothills almost everywhere. It usually has about half as many spines (4 to 10) as the other species and they are longer (nearly an inch) covered with loose-fitting, glossy, white, greenish, or brownish tipped sheaths. *Opuntia spinosior* (meaning "spinier" in comparison with *O. whipplei* with which it was originally confused) is to be seen at its best in southern Arizona but extends, as small plants mostly, into southwestern New Mexico from the Silver City region southward. At its best it is quite a tree, often 20 feet high or more, but in New Mexico it is usually a smaller plant without the tree-like form. As compared with *O. arborescens* it has many more spines (12 to 20 in the areola), the areolae are more numerous, the stem is less tuberculate, the spines are shorter (length about ½ an inch) and the sheaths fit the spines quite closely; the sheaths are a rather dirty white with a faint pinkish tinge which gives the species a characteristic appearance, easily seen by one who understands it but hard to describe accurately.

The PLATYOPUNTIAE ("flat" jointed species) constitute the most important group of cacti in New Mexico having the most species, by far the greatest number of individuals and being certainly the most economically valuable of any of the cacti as we know them today. They are the "prickly pears," or *Nopales*, the fruits being known as *tunas* by the Spanish-speaking people.   Seventeen species are here listed and it is altogether likely that further study will bring to light others not now recognized as distinct. As here treated they belong to three groups, those having dry fruits (XEROCARPAE), and those with succulent fruits, the plants being more or less erect, and those with succulent fruits in which the plants are mostly prostrate. Of the dry-fruited species (of which there are probably at least four in the state) the commonest is the little *O. polyacantha* ("many spines") (*O. missouriensis* of the older books), a small-jointed nearly prostrate plant with numerous white or yellow spines. The joints are mostly obovate (egg-shaped with the large end up) or nearly circular, the spines are slender, highly colored, and from 1 to 2 inches long, 1 to 5 in each areola with numerous small spicules. The fruit is usually short ellipsoidal with varying degrees of spininess. This is the common plant in the piñon and cedar covered areas and on the high mesas in the northern part of the state, where it forms large, irregular beds mainly on sandy soils. The other three species resemble it closely. *O. hystricina* has somewhat larger joints, 5 or 6 inches long and the spines are longer, 2 to 4 inches, and fully as numerous. (We have seen no New Mexican material of this but the original description states that it occurs west of Albuquerque.   It was described from Arizona material). The second is *O. trichophora* ("bearing hairs") and is very similar to *U. polyacantha,* except that the lower joints have numerous slender, curved and bent, hair-like, white, or dirty whitish spines and very numerous spicules. *O. sphaerocarpa* ("spherical fruit") is a nearly related species of the Sandia Mountains which has nearly circular joints about 3 inches in diameter, very wrinkly, green, and with spines only on the upper areolae; its fruits are almost spherical and have very few or no spicules. These last two named species are sometimes considered as varieties of *O. polyacantha,* which they resemble, but they are more easily separated than some of the other species of the genus and should probably be recognized as of specific rank. All these dry-fruited species have very large seeds, fully ¼ of an inch in diameter with a prominent ridge about them. They all occur mostly in the colder parts of the state and are quite abundant on some of the high sandy plains and mesas of the northern counties, at elevations above 6,000 feet.

The remaining species of the genus have succulent, fleshy fruits, tunas in Spanish, that are usually ellipsoidal or egg-shaped or nearly spherical and some shade of dull red or purple. The pulp of the fruit is greenish, reddish or purple and the seeds are disk-shaped, mostly smaller than those of the dry-fruited species and generally with narrower ridge. There are part of them (7 species) more or less erect in habit, about 2 to 5 feet high with at least 3 or 4 joints growing upward and not seeming to lie on the ground, and another part (6 species) that spread over the ground, the stems seeming too weak to hold more than about one joint off the ground, those on the ground resting mostly on edge and rooting freely.

Of the first group *O. chlorotica* ("green," in reference to the greenish yellow color of the plant produced largely by the nearly translucent uniform yellow spines) has medium joints, 6 or 8 inches long, circular to obovate, with spines ½ to 1 inch long in clusters of 3 to 5 and bent down against the face of the joint. The plant is often 4 feet high or more and frequently has a more or less conspicuous short trunk. It is one of the interesting species coming into our range from Arizona but is difficult to transplant. We have tried twice to grow it, but the cuttings failed to strike root.

Opuntia macrocentra ("large centrals") is a common species of the mesas of the southern part of the state. It has thin, reddish tinged, circular joints with very long (2 to 3 inches, or even 4 inches) black or very dark brown spines. The plant is rarely over 2½ feet high and a little inclined to spread, though rarely actually lying down. Its joints are usually about 5 or 6 inches in diameter, and the fruit a dull red with rather pleasant though insipid taste.

Opuntia dulcis ("sweet") is a name applied to some scrappy specimens received from southwestern Texas by Dr. Engelmann and not known in many of the collections today. We are not certain that our own plant belongs here but it is temporarily so referred pending further study. The fruit is quite characteristic as are the seeds, both of which were pretty carefully described and our material seems to match the descriptions in all particulars. The plant is 3 or 4 feet high with obovate joints, rather thick, pale green with few short, whitish spines; some joints with almost none, and a smooth obovate, dark purple fruit with pulp the same color, very sweet, containing many small seeds about ⅛ of an inch in diameter and with very narrow, rounded ridge. This is the plant referred to as *O. laevis* (?) from which it differs in the character of the spines and the fruit.

Opuntia phaeacantha ("brown spined") is the common, erect plant of northern New Mexico and southern Colorado, where it is nowhere very abundant. It has bright green joints, 5 or 6 inches long, obovate, with rather dark, stoutish spines, 2 inches long or less. At the higher levels it is generally small and inclined to lie on the ground. Well grown plants of the lower levels are often 3 feet high and somewhat inclined to spread. The lower smaller plants approach *O. camanchica* of the procumbent group.

Opuntia dillei (named for Mr. A. B. Dille of Alamogordo who discovered it in the Sacramento Mountains) is a very large jointed plant; the joints are thick, green, nearly circular, 10 inches or more in diameter and almost spineless. When spines occur they are stout, about one inch long, yellow mottled with reddish brown, and mostly on the areolae of the edge of the joints. The flowers are very large, ¾ of an inch or more in diameter, and the purple fruit is also large for the genus as represented in New Mexico.

Opuntia wootonii (named for the writer by Dr. Griffths) has large oval joints most of which taper somewhat towards the top, though often broadest above the middle. Its joints are usually 10 inches long or more, though the younger ones may be less. Its spines are very stout, 3 to 5 in an areola, all over the joints, on sides and edges, 1½ to 2 inches long, clear yellow on the tips, reddish brown at the base and somewhat mottled. The flower is a dark yellow, when it opens, with reddish brown markings at the base of the petals. The fruit is purple and moderately large.

Opuntia engelmanni (named for Dr. Engelmann, who studied the cacti extensively and named most of the species of the southwestern states) is perhaps the commonest large jointed, erect Opuntia in New Mexico. It has large, circular or obovate joints, 8 inches to a foot long, rather yellowish green, with fairly numerous spines. The spines are usually 1 to 2 inches long, white or whitish, 2 to 5 in the areola. Those areolae on the edge of the joints mostly have 4 or 5 spines; those on the sides 2 or rarely 3, somewhat deflexed, spreading widely on the edges and sometimse on the sides. The flowers are bright yellow when they first open;

the fruit is large, dark purple outside and inside, with rather large seeds. Dr. Engelmann named a variety *cyclodes* with small spherical fruit and circular joints from near Anton Chico, and most New Mexican material has been referred to this, we believe wrongly, for while the circular joints are common the spherical fruit we have failed so far to find. The preserved material from southern New Mexico exactly matches *O. engelmanni* material from Chihuahua, the type locality of that species. Hence, we refer our material to the species rather than the variety.

The remaining six species are all procumbent, i. e. they lie on the ground, spreading more or less and rooting wherever the joints touch. *Opuntia ballii* (named in honor of Mr. C. R. Ball, who first collected it) is a small plant with joints about 2 to 2½ inches broad, few long, slender spines, often 2 inches long, brownish or dirty white prominent yellow spicules on the upper areolae, and a slender, clavate fruit, with large, thick seeds almost as thick as broad, ¼ of an inch in diameter.

Opuntia cymochila very closely resembles some forms of *O. polyacantha,* being prostrate and spreading, having small joints covered with rather slender yellowish white spines, but the fruit is pulpy—not dry. *Opuntia tenuispina* (thin or slender spined) is one of the commoner plants of the Mesilla Valley. The plant is prostrate, the joints obovate, 5 to 7 inches long, 3 or 4 inches wide, densely covered with slender white spicules 2 inches long and more, bright yellow flowers and a rather small, ellipsoidal, red fruit with mostly greenish pulp and medium-sized seeds. It is badly attacked by the cochineal. *Opuntia filipendula* is a species named from the Mesilla Valley, but not found since.

Opuntia toumeyi (named for Prof. J. W. Toumey), *O. chihuahuaensis* (living in Chihuahua) and *O. camanchica* (after the Indians in whose land it was first found) are all three very nearly alike. They are prostrate with obovate joints 6 or 7 inches long, viciously spiny with long, stout spines and prominent yellow or brown spicules. Their flowers are mostly yellow with reddish brown markings at the bases of the petals inside, and of medium size. *O. toumeyi* has light colored spines erect on the edges of the joints and pressed down to the joints on the sides. The other two have dark brown spines 2 to 3 inches long and yellowish or brownish spicules, widely spreading in all directions. In *O. camanchica* the plants are clear green, mostly not very large and differing from *O. phaeacantha* only in habit. *O. chihuahuaensis* has joints more yellowish green and very prominent yellow or brownish spicules which are particularly abundant on the older joints especially in the marginal areolae.

MAMILLARIA.

The genus *Mamillaria* (meaning "bearing teats," in reference to the peculiar tubercles on which the spines are borne) displays about a dozen species in New Mexico. They are mostly small plants, some of them quite small indeed, and the largest single plant is hardly more than 6 inches high. Most of the species are globular or oval, a few are short cylindric. All of them are tubercled and the spine clusters consist of two kinds of spines, one or more rows of slender and smaller spines radiating more or less horizontally from the outer edges of the areolae (the radials) and a few stouter erect or divergent ones from the centers of the areolae (the centrals). In some of the species the tubercles have a groove in the upper side that is somewhat hairy or woolly, the degree of wooliness varying with the species. In one of our species this groove does not appear in the young tubercles and only reaches about half way to the apex in the mature ones. The flowers are produced just above the moderately young tubercles. As the growth of these plats takes place at the top of the stem by the formation of new tubercles which are gradually forced away from the center by further growth, and as the flowers appear in the axils of the moderately young tubercles but not the very young ones; they seem to form something like a ring about the center and near the top, but are not yet forced over on the side of the stem (the common position in the *Echinocerei*), and not crowded in the very center at the top as is more or less the habit of the *Echinocacti*. The fruit, also, is quite characteristic being entirely smooth, without scales or spines.

The genus is of no importance economically in New Mexico except for the few plants collected to be sold to the fanciers and to herbaria, hence it is not necessary to discuss them very extensively. Of the twelve species here listed we have nine growing at the college in the garden and a few of them are very interesting additions to the collection. They are practically without common names so it will be necessary to use the Latin ones. *Mamillaria micromeris* (referring to the small spines), *M. lasiacantha* (the woolly-spined maiillaria), and *M. dasyacantha* (the "erect-spined" mamillaria); all three of these are very small plants usually about 1 inch to 1½ inches in diameter and about as high, rarely two inches high or more, and covered very completely with numerous fine, white spines ⅛ to ¼ of an inch long. The flowers are small and the fruit which in one species comes long after the flowers, is narrowly club-shaped or a little broader at the top. *M. dasyacantha* normally has one central spine to each tubercle but this is often missing while the other two species never have any. It has red flowers and the tubercles are grooved, while in the other two species the flowers are pale pink or whitish and the tubercles are not grooved. To separate *M. micromeris* from *M. lasiacantha* it is necessary only to look at the spines with a lens. The last named species has spines that are covered with fine hairs and in the other they are smooth. They may easily be told almost at a glance for *M. micromeris* is flattened on top and even sunken a bit in the middle and some of the spines are much longer and spirally arranged about the depression, while *M. lasiacantha* has a rounded top and the spines are not elongated. The fruit of *M. micromeris* is about half an inch long, bright red, and comes on the plant a long time after it was in bloom. Plants collected about August 4, which had bloomed previously, produced ripe fruit in the greenhouse again in the winter.

Mamillaria grahami (Graham's mamillaria), and Wright's mamillaria (*M. Wrightii*), are two little plants that are easily recognized. They are from 1½ to 3 inches high, oval and covered with small white radial spines about ¼ of an inch long. Besides the radials the tubercles bear slightly stouter, dark colored, hooked spines about 1 inch long. In *M. grahami* there is but one hooked central in each cluster and they are dark reddish brown or sometimes a bit ashy colored, while the radial spines are so numerous as to make the plant look white or gray. *M. wrightii* has two or three hooked centrals in at least some of the clusters and they are nearly black, while the radials are not so numerous and allow the green plant beneath to show through thus making the plant appear green. The flowers of *M. wrightii* are described as about 1 inch long and bright purple. We have never seen them. Those of *M. grahami* are about the same size and bright pink, followed by a red fruit which comes later and lasts for some time.

Two other species closely related and similar to each other are

M. meiacantha ("more spines"), and *M. heyderi* (Heyder's mamillaria). They are generally larger than any of those yet mentioned and somewhat top-shaped. The part above ground is from 3 to 6 inches in diameter and nearly flat on top, rising above the level of the ground only an inch or so, while the root is much thickened above and conical, tapering to a point under ground. The tubercles are more or less 4-angled, not grooved, about ¼ to ½ an inch long and as far apart. The sap is thickish and milky, a characteristic common in the *Euphorbias,* some of which are also arid land plants, rather similar to the cacti found rather abundantly in arid Africa. The spines are of two sorts and by them the species may be recognized. In *M. meiacantha* the radials are few, from 5 to 9, dull colored, one-fourth to one-third of an inch long and moderately stiff, while the single central is generally slightly larger or often wanting. The radial spines of Heyder's mamillaria are slender and weak, white and more numerous, 10 to 20 in a cluster, and the stouter central always present. They both produce pale little flowers about an inch long and some time later small, bright red fruits appear. They are both interesting pot plants though not of much account as garden plants because they are easily covered by wind-blown sand.

The next two species are not very closely related and are here considered together because they are larger than the rest in all particulars. *Mamillaria macromeris* (referring to the large spines), produces individual plants about 5 or 6 inches tall (about half this length is usually under ground) and two inches in diameter, of cylindrical form; its tubercles are about ½ to ¾ of an inch long, grooved part way from the base; its spines are long, 1½ to 2 inches or even longer and straight, the radials are about 12 to 15 and the centrals 4 or 5. The radials are slender and whitish; the centrals spread widely, are dark brown or blackish and two inches long or more. The flowers are from 2½ to 3 inches long, opening slightly less, bright lavender to pale purple, and open in bright sunshine. They are followed by a smooth, green, egg-shaped fruit with yellowish, smooth seeds. The plants form clusters sometimes 2 to 3 feet in diameter, slightly rising in the centre forming a regular circular flower bed, which is usually very beautiful when the plants are in bloom in the summer time.

Scheer's mamillaria (*M. scheerii*) is the largest species that grows in the state, being about 6 inches tall and almost as

broad when grown. The plants are usully found growing singly
and are quite rare on the mesas of the southern part of the state.
The tubercles are flat, almost an inch long in large specimens,
conical, set rather wide apart and grooved. The spines are somewhat shorter than in the preceding species being usually about
1 inch long, light straw colored or dull, stouter and less numerous;
radials about 8 or 10 (6 to 16) and centrals 2 to 5, one of the
latter usually bent a little downward at the tip. The flowers
are most striking, being a bright bronze yellow or golden
brown almost 3 inches long and opening almost as widely in
bright sunshine. The fruit is irregularly oval tapering at the
base, light green and smooth, about 1½ inches long, with rather
large light brown seeds and no pulp.

The final group contains three species of oval or cylindrical
stemmed plants from 1½ to 6 inches high and usually 1 to 2
inches in diameter thickly beset by whitish spines about ½ an
inch long and more or less ashy or purplish or reddish brown at
the tips. One of these, *M. tuberculosa,* (the tuberculose mamillaria) usually branches considerably, forming clusters of stems
and the bases of the stems are covered by the old, corky
or woody tubercles from which the spines have fallen. It may
also be recognized by its bright red fruit which persists for some
time. Its spines are very numerous, usually ashy or slightly
purplish tipped and white at the base, while its flowers are small
(less than an inch long) and pink, usually rather pale. This
little plant is commonly found growing in crevices of limestone
and must be grown in soil containing plenty of lime or it will
die.

M. vivipara variety *borealis* is a rare little plant found so far
in but one place in the mountains in the northern part of
the state and it is not likely to be met with often.

M. radiosa, and its more common variety *neo-mexicana* (the
name of the species refers to the radiating character of the spines)
occur sparsely scattered almost everywhere in the state, especially
at elevations of 6,000 to 8,000 feet. They usually occur singly
or a few together. The spines do not fall off at the base leaving
naked tubercles. The central spines, usually 4 to 6, are often
purplish and the radials more or less reddish brown at the tip,
whitish at the base. The flowers are a bright rose pink and 1 to
1½ inches long, mostly of the smaller size. The fruit is always

green and the seeds a reddish brown. The variety *neo-mexicana* differs from the species by having more numerous spines with purplish centrals. It is the more common in the state.

ECHINOCACTUS.

The genus *Echinocactus* (meaning "hedgehog cactus") is represented in New Mexico by seven species. Of two of these we have not seen specimens collected in New Mexico although one of them was originally named from material collected at Santa Fe. This species is very rare in collections and has been reported but once since the original collection. The other specie is reported once from our extreme western boundary but we have not seen any of this material. The remaining five species we are familiar with, having collected them all in the field and having them all growing in the cactus garden. It is possible that another species or two may be found growing within the limits of the state and one is to be expected in the extreme southwestern corner that is not listed here.

All of the species of the genus are, as a matter of course, of interest to the cactus fancier, for he is interested in all the peculiar and bizarre types he can find, and the more unique they are the better for his purposes.

Of the five species that are represented in our collection three may be used as pot plants, and the other two are too large for use in anything but large urns or a bedding plants. Only one, the "visnaga," is used economically in any other way than for purposes of decoration. For use in rockeries, gardens of arid land plants, and bizarre collections of plants they are particularly effective.

Three of the species here considered have large and conspicuous flowers and bloom in the middle of the summer. Two of these are followed by conspicuous fruits which remain on for some time. One of the smaller species superficially resembles some species of Echinocereus and Mamillaria so much as to be easily mistaken for them by the careless observer. The genus may be recognized by the following characters: The plant body is ribbed by the confluence of the tubercles in vertical or slightly spiral rows; the flowers are always borne in the middle right at the top, never some distance away from the center; the flowers open in bright sunlight; the ovary and fruit are covered with scales but do not have spines, nor are they smooth; the seeds are mostly not embedded in a pulp of any kind seeming to be loose in the one-celled somewhat leathery pod.

Wright's *Echinocactus* is a medium sized plant, the fleshy stems being from 3 to 5 inches high and 2 to 3 inches or slightly more in .diameter, but armed with long, pale yellow, hooked spines that project all around it in such a way as to make it appear larger and protect it most effectively. The plant is very rare and grows among the rocks of the foothills in bunches of dried grass, just the color of the spines, which most effectively obscure it.   The spines are like a medium-sized fish hook with a very long shank and lacking the barb, the points being very sharp, and they are so arranged that as one tries to get away from one spine he is caught by another. Though moderately slender they are so strong that they can inflict a severe wound if one should try to tear away from them. The flower is small, hardly an inch long, and half as wide and does not open wide. They are borne almost in the center of the somewhat flattened top of the stem among young spines and several are produced almost together in the early spring. The flower is insignificant on account of its color, which is a peculiar dull purplish brown or almost maroon color.   While not conspicuous this color is rare in blossoms of any kind and to be coupled to this rare plant makes it all the more valuable to the fancier.

Wislizenus's *Echinocactus,* the "visnaga" or "barrel cactue" is the largest cylindrical cactus found growing in the state. Large specimens get to. be three and one-half to four feet tall and most of them are from 12 to 18 inches in diameter. The top is rounded or flattened and the ridges are moderately acute, about 1 inch high, 2 inches apart and run lengthwise of the stem or sometimes wind spirally about it. The spines are very robust; several centrals are flattened and spread in all directions; these are more or less alternately banded or ringed with dull red and yellowish white; the one upright central is strongly hooked downward. They are usually about 2 inches long though sometimes on very old plants they are as much as four inches long. Surrounding the central spines are some slender more or less bent whitish radials 2 inches long or more which weave in with those of the adjoining rows. Well grown plants of this species may weigh as much as 200 pounds and the smaller ones often weigh 50 to 75 pounds. This plant is used considerably in beds in the southern part of the state and in adjoining Texas, and is effective on account of its large size and its queer shape. It attracts attention wherever it is seen and is easily transplanted. It blooms rather late in the summer, generally in July or August, producing a dozen or so deep orange colored flowers 2 to 2½ inches long in the middle of the stem at the top. The orange colored fruit remains on the plant until the next season. The fruit is a scaly berry, which looks good enough to eat but is in reality only the leathery rind containing very many small glossy black seeds in the single other-wise empty cell. The plant was described from material collected by Dr. Wislizenus near Dona Ana in 1846, in whose honor it was named.

Besides its horticultural use, the "visnaga" is used somewhat extensively for the manufacture of a kind of candy called *cubiertas* by the Mexicans or sometimes *dulces de visnaga*. The plant is dug —an easy process since the roots are quite slender and cut off readily—and with a heavy knife the spines (ridges and all) are all cut off and the plant taken to the work shop, which is usually the home of this primitive candy maker. Here the pulpy, white interior of the stem is cut up into pieces half an inch thick and a few inches square and candied by boiling it in a sugar solution until it is rendered firm and somewhat crisp in texture and saturat-ed with sugar. It is then allowed to cool and is ready for sale, being covered all over with a coating of white crystalized sugar. It is usually sold by street venders, generally the maker, at the rate of three or four pieces for 5 cents. The cactus has a flavor of its own which it imparts to the candy; some people like it, others do not.

Some years ago Mr. Frederick W. Wright* devised a method of making a substitute for leather to be used in certain particular ways, from the fleshy pulp of the visnaga and the saguaro. Mr. P. C. Standley repeated the experiment on the fleshy interior of the *visnaga* and the piece of "leather" he made is still flexible and in good shape; it has not hardened.   It has not been subjected to an sort of wear, however, simply lying around on the table in the herbarium for two years or more; but it does not seem to have changed in any way from what it was when first completed. Mr. Wright suggested several uses to which such a product might be

---

* Plant World 1909.

put and devised methods of cutting the plant to give as large pieces of the product as might be. It is hardly likely that the manufacture of a leather substitute in this way will ever be a very important industry since the supply of raw material is quite limited and reproduces itself very slowly. We have no data at hand that will throw any light on the rate of growth of these plants but there is every reason to believe that the large plants one sees are possibly 20 or 25 years old or even older.

Echinocactus papyracanthus, (literally the ʻʻpaper spined" Echinocactus), must be a very interesting little plant and should be sought in the region of Santa Fe, where it has been found twice. It is a very small member of a genus of normally rather large plants. One would hardly recognize it as a cactus at all because its "spines" consist of flattened, flexible, papery outgrowths, not spiny at all. The stem is so tuberculate that it was first believed to be a Mamillaria. Collectors in that region should be on the lookout for it.

Echinocactus horizonthalonius is not blessed with a vernacular name though it is one of the commonest species in the southern part of the state, occurring in the crevices of the limestone rocks, which form low mountains in that region. The plant is nearly spherical except when quite old, when it is a little taller than broad. It withstands the driest of seasons and prospers in locations such as described but does not do well in soils that do not have abundance of lime in them. Plants planted on a mound 12 to 18 inches high made up largely of some slaked lime and old mortar have grown very well with much less loss than similar plants planted in the ordinary mesa soil of the garden, and treated the best way we knew how. This species is rather easily recognized; it is almost globular from 3 to 6 inches in diameter, a little flattened when young and a little elongated in age. It has a few, generally 6 or 7 rounded ridges running lengthwise on which are borne the spine clusters. The spines are quite stout, nearly round and bent in such a way as to parallel the surface of the plant. Dead plants often decay in such a fashion as to leave the network of strong spines preserving the outward semblance of the plant although it be long dead and mostly decayed. As a pot plant this species is very satisfactory for it requires but little care or protection from anything except too much water. An open, gravelly soil having plenty of limestone is very satisfactory to it. Its size makes it convenient for pot culture and it does particularly well in rockeries which supply the root conditions which it requires. It blooms quite profusely in the middle of the summer, each well grown plant producing from 3 to 6 large bright pink blossoms that open in bright sunlight and close at night. The blossoms are about 3 inches long and the corolla opens about that amount. They usually bloom two days, at least, fading somewhat the second day. The base of the flower is thickly covered by white, woolly hairs that completely cover and hide the fruit which follows. It is a very good bloomer and flowers in the middle of the summer at a time when many of the other species are through blooming.

The "Devil's Pincushion" (*Echinocactus texensis*) (its Latin name means the Echinocactus that dwells in Texas) is a rather striking plant that comes into the eastern part of the state from Texas. It is low, 6 inches high or usually much less in the specimens we have seen, and 10 inches to a foot or more in diameter with a dozen or more acute ridges radiating from the center at the top. On the ridges are the clusters of stout spines, which spread widely following somewhat the curve of the stem's surface. The spines are more or less ringed, red and white, and are somewhat flattened. They are mostly about 1½ inches long but do not overlap as much as in the preceding species. It is of no value except for decorative purposes, but in a region where there is so little water as in New Mexico, it is a valuable addition to a very restricted flora. The queer, flat-topped, dark green plant with its stout spines and its large, pale pink flowers with rather woolly bases is certainly worth cultivating in a garden devoted to such vegetation as is common in New Mexico. The fruit too is a bright red and the rind is succulent, not tough, and is embedded in a tuft of white woolly hairs. The fruit lasts about a week. The plant blooms in the early summer.

Echinocactus intertextus (the name having reference to the way the spines are woven together) is a small plant of the mesas and foothills of the southern part of the state. It is thickly covered with short, straight, white spines ½ to ¾ of an inch long, some of which are ashy gray at the tip. The plant is rarely over four inches high and 2½ inches in diameter and the spines are so thickly set that one cannot see the stem beneath the covering. The flowers are small, a pale pink and come about the first of any cactus in the spring. The fruit is merely a small, dry "berry" with several seeds. The plant is of convenient size for growing in pots and it has long been known and used for that purpose.

ECHINOCEREUS.

The genus *Echinocereus* is economically one of very little importance in New Mexico nothwithstanding the dozen or more species which are widely distributed all over the state in one form or another. They are, generally speaking, somewhat larger than the Mamillarias and not so large as some of more conspicuous species of the Echinocacti. They practically all have cylindrical stems though a few are so short as to be oval and none of them are very tall, rarely exceeding a foot in height. And they are most of them quite spiny, each in its own way, and a few of them very spiny indeed. The stems are usually about 3 inches in diameter and have from 6 or 7 to 12 or 14 more or less sharp ridges running lengthwise, upon which are spine-bearing areolae. A few of the species are usually found as single stems, but most of them grow in clusters of from 2 or 3 stems up to a dozen or 20. Two of the species form large groups often containing 50 or more stems in the cluster. When these plants are dug up they are seen to be all from a single primary root. Such plants in bloom form veritable flower beds, for they are profuse bloomers. The spines of the Echinocerei are very variable in size, color, and number in the areolae, and must be considered in any plan for determining the species; some of them are highly colored and add much to the beauty of the plant. The flowers of the different species vary much both in size and in color; the smallest are about ¾ to 1 inch long and do not open very wide, while the largest are 3 to 3½ inches long, or rarely more, and when completely open are almost as wide as they are long. The colors displayed are green, yellow, rose color, scarlet, red, and various shades of purple. White-flowered species or those which are a clear blue we do not have. The flowers are borne on the ridge between the spine-bearing areloae and above areolae of the previous season, thus placing them on the side of the stem, not in the middle at the top as is common in two other genera. Another easily recognized character lies in the spine-covered base of the flower and the fruit. These spines are always weaker than those of the stems and when the fruit is ripe may be easily brushed off; in some cases they even fall off themselves, and this is a good way to tell when the fruit is ripe. The fruit has a

thin rind and the interior is filled with crisp, whitish pulp, full of
the small, mostly black, and finely tuberculate seeds. It is generally
greenish outside or dull yellowish with a reddish brown area. They
are pleasantly tart to the taste and are the most palatable of any of
the fruits of the native cacti, having a flavor suggestive of "ground
cherries." One species is locally known as "strawberry" cactus
because of a fancied resemblance in the taste of the fruit.

The plants of this genus are very satisfactory for bedding purposes since they are easily transplanted and most of them bloom
very freely. They are rarely so large but that they can be grown
as pot plants and they are so hardy as to succeed well in most
situations where they get sufficient sunlight and not too much
water. All the species here listed will grow readily outside in
New Mexico without protection at places where the minimum winter
temperature is not lower than 0°F. Some of the species will
doubtless stand still lower temperature without serious damage.
A few of them are to be found well up on the mountains of the
northern part of the state where the winter temperatures are
pretty low. The species of the *coccineus* group are used as bedding
plants quite freely by the people of the southern part of the state
and are very satisfactory for the purpose, especially for rockeries
or for gardens whose owners try to grow the native plants of the
region. For convenience of identification they are most readily divided into groups on the basis of the size and color of the flowers,
and the species may then be separated by spine characters.

The first group is that having green flowers (the specific names
both mean green flowered, one derived from Greek the other from
Latin) and contain two species. The flowers of these little plants
are about an inch long and the dull greenish petals do not spread
open but stand almost erect, the flowers being mostly about half an
inch wide at the top. They open only in bright sunlight. The plants
of this group are very thickly covered with spines and the spines
are variegated in color, some red and some white and some particolored. *Echinocereus chloranthus* is the taller of the two, usually
6 or 8 inches high when well grown, about 1½ to 2 inches in
diameter with a rather pointed apex and its flowers appear well
down on the sides of the stem. The plant is sometimes branched but
not often and it much prefers a limestone soil, it being common on
all the low limestone hills and mountains of the southern part of
the state. It is most easily recognized by its spines. The radials

are much crowded and spread outward and upward in every direction and are very much interlocked; they are usually ½ to ¾ of an inch long. The centrals (3 to 6) are always conspicuous on older plants (sometimes wanting on young ones) and one of them stands straight up from the areaola, (said to be erect) and some of them are often slightly curved. The species was first collected on the mountains near El Paso. *Echinocereus viridiflorus* is the common green flowered species of the northern part of the state where it is usually a small plant, rarely over 3 or 4 inches high and mostly with but a single oval stem. It is usually 2 inches or more in diameter and flattened at the top. Its radial spines are rarely over ½ an inch long and spread in such a way as to seem pressed against the plant. The ridges are low and most of the areolae are without central spines, a relatively large percentage of the plants showing no centrals at all. The centrals. when present, are shorter and stouter and there is only one or rarely a second slender one in each areola. In the southern part of the state there is a form of the species (known as variety *tubulosus*) which is larger, often branched and with centrals more often present.

There are five species of large flowered Echinocerei growing in New Mexico all of which are well worth cultivation on account of the great beauty of their flowers. Three of them have short, rigid spines aranged in nearly straight rows on each side of the oblong areolae, nearly parallel to each other, and pressed against the plant. (They are said to be "pectinate" because of their resemblance to little combs); the central spines are almost always wanting and if present are short and stout. Of these three *E. dasyacanthus* ("erect" spines) has most beautiful lemon yellow flowers with a spread of over 3 inches. The plants are mostly single-stemmed though sometimes sparsely branched, the stem being about 6 or 8 inches (old plants sometimes 10 inches or more) and about 3 inches in diameter; the top of the stem is somewhat flattened. The spines are very numerous, white or whitish, almost completely concealing the stem, and tipped with pinkish gray, so the plant has a faint pink tinge. The "Rainbow Cactus," *E. rigidissimus* (referring to the "very rigid" spines) is a plant closely resembling the preceding in shape, size, and spinal arrangement, but its spines are variegated red and white and arranged somewhat in bands of the different colors or mottled about the stems. Its flower is perhaps the most beautiful of any kind of the genus, being a rich, rose color and as large as that of *E. dasyacanthus*. Its particolored spines are but an added beauty to the plant. Dealers and fanciers know it under the common name given and prize it highly as a pot plant. The little plant here referred to as *Echinocereus pectinatus* ("pectinate" or comb-like spines) is probably a species as yet undescribed, and is referred but temporarily to that species until it can be further studied. It is only 3 or 4 inches high and about 2 inches in diameter, simple or sparingly branched at the base, rounded but not flattened at the top. Its radial spines are white, about one-fourth to one-third of an inch long and the centrals are wanting. The flower is about 3 inches long and slightly less in diameter when spread, and of a bluish purple color. All three of the species above described are rare in New Mexico. *E. dasyacanthus* (originally named from El Paso) is to be found only in the extreme southern part of the state being fairly common in the region of Carlsbad. *E. rigidissimus* is known only from the extreme southwestern corner of the state where it is rare. It is common in certain localities of southern Arizona and northern Sonora. The little *E. pectinatus* comes into eastern Eddy county from the Staked Plains region of Texas.

The other two large flowered species of Echinocereus both have purple flowers but are quite different in appearance both from each other and from the species already named. Fendler's Echinocereus, *E. fendleri*, (named for its collector August Fendler, who collected at Santa Fe in 1847) is a rather small or medium sized plant in clusters of 2 to 6 (or sometimes more) stems, about 8 or 10 inches high and 1½ to 2 inches in diameter, with oval apex and rather numerous spines. The radials (mostly 7 in an areola) are from ½ to 1 inch long, variable in color, dirty white or gray or brown; they differ considerably in length and stand out at various angles. The single central is usually stout, from a thickened base and is from 1 to 2 inches long and vertically erect, the upper ones being somewhat incurved towards each other; they are nearly always darkish or dark brown at tips. *Echinocereus stramineus* ("straw colored," referring to the spines) is densely covered with long, yellow or straw-colored spines, the younger upper ones being a smoky brown at first. It is always in clusters and the old plants form oval or hemispherical beds a foot high and often 3 feet in diameter containing 50 or more stems. The individual stems are generally very noticably ribbed and sometimes have a somewhat shriveled apperance. . The spines consist of mostly 8 radials (7 to 14) ¾ to 1¼ inches long, widely divergent and covering the plant completely. This plant also seems to be very particular that there be abundance of lime in the soil it grows in. It is ordinarily found most abundantly on limestone hills and low mountains in the southern part of the state.

The last group to be mentioned is perhaps the best represented in the state and is to be distinguished by the size and color as well as some other peculiarities of its flowers. The flowers of this group are mostly or medium size for the genus, being from 1½ to about 2 inches long, rarely reaching a length of three inches. They vary from a bright orange scarlet to a deep cardinal red, never blue or purple. Occasionally the petals are or fade into a rose color. The species of the previously mentioned groups have flowers that open in bright sunlight and close up at night, while those of this group remain open day and night from the time they open until they wither. Their petals. also, are a little thicker and waxier than those of the preceding groups and they are mostly rounded and blunt, rarely ever being acute.

Of the seven species listed here, two have very stout spines that are not rounded but are sharply angled. These spines are usually not very numerous in the areolae and vary from ¾ to 1¼ inches as an average length. Of the two species *E. gonacanthus* (meaning "angled spines") has usually about 6 spines in an areolae, its upper centrals are frequently almost black and as much as 2 inches long. *E. triglochidiatus* (meaning "three spined") usually has only 3 spines in each areola and they are slightly shorter and less stout. Excepting the difference in the spines the two species look very much alike. Their stems are cylindrical, 2½ to 3½ inches in diameter, from 8 inches to about a foot high (under very favorable circumstances the first named species is two feet high), and sparingly branched, generally consisting of 2 to 4 or 5 stems, though sometimes forming a cluster of 25 or 30 as in the figure. The spines are so few that they do not hide the stems which are dark green and succulent with rather few (6 or 7) prominent ridges. The flowers are generally a dark "cardinal" red (quite frequently described as crimson in the books, mostly because the authors do not know what crimson is) and they are produced in moderate abundance only.

The remaining species of the group are very closely alike only one of them being easily separable from the rest. This is *E. pauci-*

spinus which is to be distinguished by the characteristic indicated
in the name i. e., it has "few spines," generally about four (3 to 6)
radials and no centrals (sometimes one). The spines of all five
of these species are not nearly so stout as are those of the two named
above but are still quite rigid and most of them are round (some of
them rather obscurely angled). They all have cylindrical stems 6 to
10 inches high with 5 to 7 ribs in *E. paucispinus,* and from 7 to 13
(mostly 11) in the others. They all branch more or less, forming
clusters of from three or four to a dozen stems, and *E. coccineus*
(meaning "red" in reference to the flowers) sometimes forms
large groups with 100 or more stems. The flowers of all are usually
a bright orange scarlet but are exceedingly variable in size and shade
of color within the rather uncertain limits of the species. Excluding
E. paucispinus the other four are very spiny, having from 8 to 16
(mostly 10 or 12) radials and 3 to 5 or 6 (mostly 4) central
spines in each areola. The spines are usually ¾ of an inch long
or more and divergent, forming a very formidable armor for the
plant. The species are so nearly alike that it is very difficult to
separate them. *E. neomexicanus* has small flowers (for the
group) about 1½ inches long and mostly 6 centrals and with
petals a little narrowed above. *E. coccineus* has rounded stems at
the top with shorter (¾ of an inch) mostly yellow spines (4
centrals), while in contrast is *E. conoideus* ("conical") having a
more tapering or conical apex to the stem with darker colored and
longer spines and somewhat larger flowers; the spines are about
the same number in the areola but are most of them an inch or more
long and the centrals are sometimes fully two inches long, dirty
brown, slender, slightly angled and a little bent. The three
last named species and another with stouter spines intermediate
in most of its characters between *E. coccineus* and *E. conoideus* have
all been going under the name of *E. polyacanthus,* a species originally named from plants collected near Chihuahua in 1846 and
recently discovered in that region by Dr. J. N. Rose. The species
of southern New Mexico will be described in a forthcoming publi-
cation.

PENIOCEREUS.

DEERHORN CACTUS (*Peniocereus greggii*). This is a species to
please the cactus fancier, first because of its rarity and second because it is a "night blooming" cereus with very beautiful and
delicate white flowers that open only at dusk and close with the

dawn. When once established they grow very well in dry soil, with a little extra water, in the warmer valleys and on the mesas at the southern edge of the state. The author has had some bloom in the cactus garden at the Experiment Station. The only specimen he ever collected died when transplanted, but plants from southwest Texas did well. The species may be recognized by the slender, generally quadranguar, grayish green stem, with spines that are mere points in small areoles along the angle of the stem which are hardly to be called ribs; the stems are a foot or so high, about a inch in diameter and sparingly branched; the color, shape, size, and the small spines suggest the name, from the fancied resemblance to deer antlers, especially when "in the velvet."

In digging up a plant for resetting care should be taken to get the large beet-like or spindle shaped root which is often six or eight inches long and 2 or 3 inches in diameter. The beautiful white flower is generally 6 inches long or more, narrowly funnel-shaped, and with numerous white petals. Like most of the species it prefers a rather loose, open soil. It probably will not endure winters more severe than those in the lower valleys and mesas at the southern end of the state, where winter temperatures sometimes go down to 0°F. or even colder.

CACTACEAE L.

The Cactus Family

Green, fleshy-stemmed, spiny, perennial plants, mostly leafless, adapted to very dry situations, and of peculiar aspect. The stems spherical, cylindric, flattened, tuberculate, ridged, or jointed; the spines and spicules borne on restricted areas known as areolæ. The flowers mostly conspicuous and quite beautiful. Sepals numerous, in several rows, becoming petal-like in the inner rows. Petals also numerous, always of delicate texture and beautiful color. Stamens very numerous often 100 or more, sensitive to touch in some genera. Ovary inferior (i. e. under all the other parts, which are grown to it) with one thick style and several stigmas. Fruit a dry or pulpy "berry" with a more or less leathery thickened rind and numerous seeds in a single cell.

The Use of the Keys.

The Keys are constructed so that the user may decide whether the plant he wishes to know the name of posesses one or the other of *two* sets of characters. If the user does not know the genera at sight he should refer to the Key to the genera under the subdivision labeled "Cactaceae. The Cactus Family." Here he must decide whether the plant bears leaves on the young stems or not; whether the stems are jointed or not; whether the spines are barbed or not, and so on through the list of characters. If his plant is without leaves, he settles the next question and follows up each pair of characters until he is at last led to the generic name of the plant he has in hand. The correct generic name having been determined, he then turns to the key of the species under that generic name and again follows through the list of characters given in the Key until he is led to the specific name. Following the Key comes a statement of the distribution of each species of the genus, each one being numbered as it is in the Key. For example; if the plant has rudimentary leaves, or jointed stems or barbed spines or the tube of the flower above the ovary is very short the plant belongs to the genus Opuntia, genus number 1, page _______ On referring to this page the reader will first find a description setting forth all the characteristics of that genus with some one of which in each category his plant should agree, and then follows a Key to the species. The joints are clavate, cylindric, or tumid or they are flattened, the pairs of characters to select from being arranged in paragraphs beginning the same distance from the left side of the page, those subdivisions beginning further to the right to be considered each in order *after* the one to the left has been decided. If our plant has joints that are either clavate, tumid or cylindric then take the next set of possibilities "Joints clavate or tumid &c"—or "Joints cylindric, more or less tuberculate" &c., and so on in order until the species name is reached, as say 5 *O. clavata.* We then refer to the number 5 of the list following and learn that *Opuntia clavata* (named by Engelmann) is "Quite common on the mesas" &c, in the Upper Sonoran Zone. The illustrations should then be examined for additional information. These data all put together and the discussion of the species under its name in the body of the bulletin should, give a fairly correct idea of the name of the species. In a short time skill in using the Keys will be obtained and even the novice may be able to make very correct determinations in so limited a number of plants. The Keys apply only to the cacti known to grow native in New Mexico and there is the possibility that some have been omitted though all possible care has been taken to avoid so doing.

The few technical terms here used can be found defined in any botanical glossary or in the dictionary. The fewest number possible have been used.

1. OPUNTIA Mill.

PRICKLY PEAR. CANE CACTUS, ETC.

Plants with jointed stems bearing small cylindrical or conical fleshy leaves that fall early from the young joints and the bases of the flowers; the joints of the stems flattened (then called "leaves" by the unobservant) (the "prickly pears" or "nopales,") cylindric (the "cane cacti" or "chollas" in part), club-shaped or swelled, slightly or not all to strongly tuberculate; leaves usually less than half an inch long, seen only on the young joints and young flowers, falling off very easily; areoles with more or less numerous retrorsely barbed bristles that separate from the plant very easily, and 1 to several slender or stout, long or short, cylindric or variously flattened or angled spines (in some species these spines are wanting); flowers large from, 1 to 3 inches long and of almost as great a diameter, with several greenish or yellowish sepals, several yellow, orange or purple, broad petals, numerous stamens, and a single style with several stigmas; fruit with or without tubercles, with several (30 or less) spicule bearing areolæ, (sometimes with a few small spines), sometimes proliferous, dry or berry-like, with a thick rind with numerous seeds in a pulpy interior; seeds rather large, ¼ of an inch in diameter or less, roughly diskshaped, with a marginal ridge around the outside edge, more or less woody, light colored. The berry like fruits are called "tunas" or "prickly pears."

The genus is a large one with many extremely variable species or a very large number of very closely related species, difficult of distinction. In New Mexico there are from 25 to 30 recognized species some of which are very local in their distribution while others are widely distributed over this state and others adjacent.

There are at least four groups of species or divisions of the genus which may be readily recognized even by the novice. They are (1) the PLATYOPUNTIAE or flat jointed Opuntias commonly called "prickly pears" or "nopales;" (2) the CYLINDROPUNTIAE or cylindrical stemmed species, the larger tree like forms of which are called "cane cacti" or "chollas" and the slender stemmed forms called "tasajillas" in Mexico; (3) the CLAVATAE or those species having thickened club shaped joints and dry fruits densely covered with circular radiating rosettes of bristles; and (4) the TUMIDAE, a small group of rare species (in New Mexico) of plants with very small joints that are swelled or thickened when growing but otherwise closely like the flat-jointed species and resembling them very much when dry.

Key to the Genera.

Plants with small thickened leaves without proper blade, which fall off when young or by the time the joints are mature; stems jointed; spines barbed: tube of the flower, above the ovary, short.

1. OPUNTIA

Plants without leaves of any kind; stems not jointed; spines not barbed; tube of the flower more or less elongated.

Stems short, mostly ovoid, spherical, or short cylindric, tuberculate; ovary and fruit smooth, neither scaly nor spiny.

2. MAMILLARIA

Stems mostly short cylindric, ovate or occasionally spherical, mostly larger than in the preceding group; tubercles confluent into longitudinal, sometimes spiral, ridges; ovary and fruit not smooth.

Ovary and fruit scaly, not spiny: flowers borne in the center at the top of the stem.

3. ECHINOCACTUS

Ovary and fruit spiny; flowers borne on the sides of the stems some distance from the top.

Flowers colored, various shades of red, yellow, green or purple, never white, blooming in bright sunlight; stems very spiny; ridges 6 or more.

4. ECHINOCEREUS

Flowers white, long and slender, opening at night only; stems slender, mostly 4 or 5 ribs; spines very short and inconspicuous,

5. PENIOCEREUS

Joints clavate, tumid or cylindric, not conspicuously flattened.

Joints clavate or tumid; plants low usually less than a foot high, spreading; spines without sheaths.

Joints tumid when fresh, simulating some forms of the Platyopuntiae when dry, very small, 1 to 2 inches long, about 1 inch wide and nearly as thick; tubercles not conspicuous; bristles of the fruit merely spreading. (TUMIDAE)

Joints circular or short obovate, about 1 inch long; bristles few. (In the mountains in the northwestern part)

1. *O. brachyarthra.*

Joints elliptic obovate, 1½ to 2 inches long and a little more than half as wide; bristles and spines very numerous, the latter small and white. (In the Rio Grande Valley at the very southern end of the state.)

2. *O. arenaria.*

Joints clavate (in one species almost cylindric), tubercles conspicuous: bristles of the fruit in radiating rosettes covering the fruit.

(CLAVATAE)

Joints large, 4 inches long or more and over an inch in thickness, strongly tuberculate; spines 1½ to 2 inches long, yellowish brown, flattened, stout: plant forming beds covering 10 square feet or more.

3. *O. emoryi.*

Joints smaller, rarely over two inches long and less than an inch thick; spines various, not yellowish brown.

Spines 1½ to 2 inches long, slender; cylindric, ashy gray; joints
about half an inch in diameter; plant forming small
clusters about a foot in diameter.

4. *O. grahami.*

Spines shorter, the longest rarely an inch long, flattened,
white, tapering from base to point, bent sharply
downward against the stem; stem thicker and
pronouncedly club-shaped; plants forming rounded
beds covering 10 square feet or more.

5. *O clavata.*

Joints cylindric, more or less strongly tuberculate; spines enclosed in a
papery sheath; plants two feet high or more. (CYLINDROPUNTIAE)
Plants about two feet high, spreading; stems from ½ to ¾ of an inch in
diameter; flowers yellow.

Sheaths of the spines pale yellowish to white; western New
Mexico and Arizona.

6. *O. whipplei.*

Sheaths of the spines yellowish brown; eastern New Mexico and
adjoining Texas.

7. *O. davisii.*

Plants taller branching from a single or a few main stems, 3 to 10 feet
high or even more; flowers purple (except in *O. leptocaulis.*)
Stems slender, mostly less than ½ inch in diameter; plant about
3 feet high when full grown; spines long and slender, 1 to
1½ inches long, 1 to 3 in an areola.

Fruit small, hardly ½ inch long, a scarlet berry, smooth
though spiny: flowers small and yellow; spines
spreading.

8. *O. leptocaulis.*

Fruit larger, about 1 inch long, dry, green with a dull reddish
tinge on one side, somewhat tuberculate: flower
dull greenish purple; spines somewhat deflexed.

9. *O. kleiniae.*

Stem stout, about 1 inch in diameter or more; plants more or less
tree like when full grown, 10 feet high or more; spines
numerous in each areola; flowers bright purple: fruit tuberculate, dry or leathery and yellow when ripe.
Spines ¾ to 1 inch long, 4 to 10 in a cluster: tubercles large and
pronounced; sheaths loose, shining, white below,
brown-tipped giving stem a whitish tinge.

10. *O. arborescens.*

Spines less than ½ an inch long, 12 to 20 in an areola; tubercles
mostly not conspicuous; sheaths close fitting, rarely
conspicuous; spines giving a decided pinkish tinge
to the stem.

11. *O. spinosior.*

Joints flattened, becoming orbicular, ovate, obovate or elliptic, several times as
wide as thick; our species all have yellow flowers, turning darker the
second day.   (PLATYPOUNTIAE.)
Fruit dry, not succulent; seeds large; plants prostrate and spreading; spines
light colored and numerous (except in *O. sphaerocarpa*); joints small
to medium size, 2 to 4 or sometimes 5 inches long.

(XEROCARPAE.)

Spines long and very numerous, 1½ to 4 inches long, 5 to 8 large ones in
each areola.

12. *O. hystricina.*

Spines shorter and less numerous, 1 to 2 inches long or even less, 1 to 5 larger ones in each areola.

Joints green, rather strongly tuberculate wrinkled; spines few, in the upper areolae only, mostly less than 1 inch long; lower part of joints mostly naked; fruit sphaeroidal.

13. *O. sphaerocarpa.*

Joints paler, mostly obscured by spines, not noticeably tuberculate and wrinkled only when dry; spines mostly covering the joints, largest often 2 inches long, a little stouter, yellowish or brownish tinged: fruit longer than broad.

Lower spines hairlike and bent, especially on the older joints and when dry.

14. *O. trichophora.*

Lower spines not hairlike, stouter; otherwise like the preceding.

15. *O polyacantha.*

Fruit succulent, with a thick rather tough rind surrounding the pulpy interior containing the seeds; seeds mostly smaller than in the preceding section: fruit mostly red or purple; joints mostly larger (small in two species); spines and habit various.

Plants with an upright habit, 2½ feet high or more, usually without any proper trunk and branching from several basal joints that are on the ground, the stems at least 3 or 4 joints high.

Spines pale yellow, uniform in color throughout, ½ to 1 inch long, 3 to 5 in an areola, bent downward against the joint: spicules same color as a spines; stems sometimes with a noticeable though short trunk.

16. *O. chlorotica.*

Spines not as defined, in previous section: spicules usually of a different color from the spines: stem never in the form of a trunk.

Joints mostly reddish colored, and thin, circular in outline, 4 to 5 inches in diameter, armed with long rather slender dark brown or black spines, (sometimes the spines are entirely absent), and brown spicules; plant usually about 2½ to 3 feet high, young ones smaller and inclined to have the habit of the next section.

19. *O. macrocentra.*

Joints never reddish, mostly yellowish green or paler: spines brown, yellow, white or variegated: spicules mostly yellowish.

Joints prevailingly obovate in form, of medium size, the joints of the year mostly about 6 to 8 inches long, older ones sometimes larger.

Spines few, short, white or pale yellow, somewhat reflexed; seeds small, barely ⅛ of an inch in diameter; fruit very sweet; rare in the southern part of the state.

18. *O. dulcis.*

Spines more numerous and longer, 1½ to 2 inches long, (in typical form on young joints the spines are dark brown,) spreading; seeds about 1/5 of an inch in diameter: the common suberect species of the north central part of the state.

19. *O. phaeacantha.*

Joints prevailingly ovate to circular in outline, (younger ones sometimes broadly obovate,) large sized, 8 to 12 inches long, old joints sometimes 18 inches long or even more in some of the species, (the largest prickly pears in the state.)

Joints ovate or elliptic, distinctly narrower at the top; spines large, stout, widely spreading, 1½ to 2 inches long, clear yellow at the tip, reddish brown at the base; spicules numerous, half an inch long or less, yellow.

20. *O. wootonii.*

Joints mostly circular in outline, sometimes a little broader above the middle in young joints or below in old ones; spines various, as are the spicules.

Spines few, on some joints none, when present yellow or brownish at the base, ½ to ¾ inch long; joints thick and succulent, rather bright green.

21. *O. dillei.*

Spines numerous, 2 to 5 in an areola, 1 to 2 inches long, spreading, the two lower often deflexed and pressed against the joint, somewhat flattened, whitish or pale.

22. *O. engelmanni.*

Plants low, mostly spreading over the ground, the joints rooting where they touch the ground, only one or two end joints trying to stand erect, mostly less than 1 foot high, sometimes forming irregular beds covering several square feet. (Compare 23 and *O. macrocentra* of the previous section which is sometimes low and spreading.)

Spines mostly white or pale, at most yellow or yellowish brown at base or tip; joints small, 6 inches or mostly about 3 or 4 inches long.

Plant small, usually consisting of only a few joints and not widely spreading; joints 2½ to 3 inches long; spines slender, 2 inches long or a little less; spicules yellow, noticeably long on the edges of young joints; fruit clavate smooth.

23. *O. ballii.*

Plants larger, of numerous joints 3 to 5 or sometimes 6 inches long; spines various; spicules usually not prominent on young joints, very numerous on the sides of old joints.

Spines usually 1 to 1½ inches long, yellowish brown at the base; plant resembling *O. polyacantha* in habit but with succulent fruit; some of the joints nearly circular, 3 to 4 inches long; seeds large, ¼ inch in diameter; roots fibrous.

24. *O cymochila.*

Spines usually 1½ to 2½ inches long, slender, mostly white; joints narrowly obovate, 4 to 6 inches long, or often longer; seeds smaller, about 1/6 of an inch in diameter.

25. *O. tenuispina.*

<blockquote>
Spines darker, stouter, light brown or dark brown, sometimes lighter at the tip or with age: joints mostly about 6 inches long or sometimes longer, obovate, sometimes broadly so, or older joints sometimes circular. (The three species here included are very much alike and separable with difficulty if properly separable at all.

Spines yellowish brown at the base, ligher toward the tip, spines on the sides of the joints usually lighter colored and more or less deflexed and appressed.

26. *O. toumeyi.*

Spines darker, mostly dark brown, widely spreading 2 to 2½ inches long or even more, rarely if ever appressed.

Spicules very abundant, especially on old joints, greenish brown to chestnut colored, about half an inch long; plant of the southern part of the state.

27. *O. chihuahuaensis.*

Spicules less numerous and shorter, generally chestnut brown or darker; plant of the central part of the state.

28. *O. camanchica.*
</blockquote>

1. Opuntia brachyarthra Engelm. and Bigel. This little plant was named from material collected at Inscription Rock in 1853 by Dr. Bigelow. It has not been collected in that region since and all other similar material so far found in the state is probably correctly referred to *O. fragilis* (Nutt.) Haw., a very similar if not the same species. If they should prove to be the same *O. fragilis* will be the proper name to apply since it is the older one. This latter species is a more northerly plant and comes into the state at the extreme northern boundary. In the upper sonoran and transition zones.

2. Opuntia arenaria Engelm. Known only from the Mesilla Valley in the extreme southern part of the state where it is rare: in the lower sonoran zone. Growing in the College cactus garden.

3. Opuntia emoryi Engelm. Known from the sandy arroyos and mesas on the extreme western edge of the state just east of Duncan Arizona, where it is quite abundant: in the lower sonoran zone.

4. Opuntia grahami Engelm. This species is not recorded from New Mexico but is very common at El Paso and in all probability will be found on the mesas in the southern part of the state; in the lower sonoran zone.

5. Opuntia clavata Engelm. Quite common on the mesas and plains and to some extent in the foothills from Socorro northward; in the upper sonoran zone. Growing in the College cactus garden.

6. Opuntia whipplei Engelm. Fairly common on the plains of the western part of the state from near Rito Quemado to the northern boundary, coming into New Mexico from Arizona; in the upper sonoran zone. Growing in the College cactus garden.

7. Opuntia davisii Engelm. & Bigel. Found on the plains of the state south of the Canadian, coming into New Mexico from Texas.

8. Opuntia leptocaulis DC. "Tasajilla." Fairly common on the mesas and in the arroyos of the southern part of the state; in the lower sonoran zone. Growing in the College cactus garden.

9. Opuntia kleiniae DC. The plant referred doubtfully to this occurs on the mesas bordering the Rio Grande from San Antonio southward, where it is not very common and is probably confused with the preceding which it resembles superficially; in the lower sonoran zone. Growing in the cactus garden.

10. Opuntia arborescens Engelm. Cane Cactus. Candelabrum Cactus. Velas de coyote. The common "tree cactus" of the state, found commonly on mesas and plains and in the foothills almost throughout the state; in the sonoran zones. Growing in the College cactus garden.

11. Opuntia spinosior (Engelm. & Bigel.) Toumey. One of the "Chollas" of southern Arizona which extends into the western part of New Mexico south of the middle; in the upper sonoran zone. Growing in the cactus garden.

12. Opuntia hystricina Engelm. This plant possibly occurs in the west central part of the state in the region of Gallup or Zuni. It is accredited to New Mexico in the original description, but the plants actually described came from Arizona. It has not been found since in New Mexico.

13. Opuntia sphaerocarpa Engelm. & Bigelow. Known only from the Sandia mountains where it is fairly common; in the upper sonoran zone. Growing in the cactus garden at the Agricultural College.

14. Opuntia trichophora (Engelm.) Britt. & Rose. Possibly not sufficiently distinct from the next, with which it is commonly associated on the mesas and plains of the northern part of the state; in the upper sonoran zone. Growing in the College cactus garden.

15. Opuntia polyacantha Haw. (*O. missouriensis* of older authors.) The commonest species on the plains and mesas of the northern part of the state, often extending into the foothills under the cedars and piñons; in the upper sonoran zone. Growing in the cactus garden.

16. Opuntia chlorotica Engelm. & Bigel. Found only in the southern and southwestern part of the state reaching as far east as the Doña Ana mountains; in the sonoran zones.

17. Opuntia macrocentra Engelm. Common on the mesas and in the arroyos of southern New Mexico; in the lower sonoran zone. Growing in the cactus garden.

18. Opuntia dulcis Engelm. The plant here referred to is in cultivation and a common escape in the Mesilla Valley. It also grows wild in Guadalupe Mountains west of Carlsbad. The uncertainty as to the name lies in the fact that the original description was from such scanty material that it is difficult to be sure what species was really named; in the lower sonoran zone. Growing, from both stations in the cactus garden.

19. Opuntia phaeacantha Engelm. This is the common suberect brown-spined species with moderately large joints found in the mountains and on the plains of the northern part of the state; in the upper sonoran and transition zones. Growing in the cactus garden.

20. Opuntia wootonii Griffiths. Known so far only from the Organ Mountains; about the lower limit of the upper sonoran zone. Growing in the cactus garden.

21. Opuntia dillei Griffiths. Known only from the Sacramento Mountains southeast of Alamogordo; in the upper sonoran zone. Growing in the cactus garden.

22. Opuntia engelmanni Salm. The commonest of the erect large-jointed species of "prickly pears" growing on the mesas and in the foot hills of the southern part of the state; in the upper sonoran zone near its lower limit. Growing in the cactus garden.

23. Opuntia ballii Rose. A peculiar little "prickly pear" from western Texas that extends into the southeastern part of New Mexico; in the sonoran zones. Growing in the cactus garden.

24. Opuntia cymochila Engelm. & Bigel. On the plains and mesas of the eastern and southeastern part of the state mainly east of the Pecos; in the sonoran zones. Growing in the cactus garden.

25. Opuntia tenuispina Engelm. The plants here referred to occur in the valleys and on the mesas in the heavier soils in the southern part of the state; in the lower sonoran zone. Growing in the College cactus garden.

26. Opuntia toumeyi Rose. On low rocky hills and in the foothills of the mountains of the southern and southwestern part of the state; in the sonoran zones. Growing in the cactus garden.

27. Opuntia chihuahuaensis Rose. On low mountains and mesas of the south central part of the state as far north as Ancho; in the sonoran zones. Growing in the cactus garden.

28. Opuntia camanchica Engelm. & Bigel. Doubtfully separable from the preceding but here relating to the plant common about Tucumcari and southward; in the upper sonoran zone.

Several other named species have been referred to the New Mexico region, one or two of which were originally described from plants collected in the state, but there is so much uncertainty as to what these names apply to in the present state of our knowledge that the author has left them out of this list. There are a few other species named from regions adjacent to our borders which have not yet been actually collected in New Mexico but which doubtless come in. One or two of this kind have been included in the list.

The present treatment of the genus Opuntia is unsatisfactory as being "neither fish nor flesh." There are either a large number more species than are here indicated or a considerable number less. The author is of the former opinion, but the plants have not yet been sufficiently studied to characterize these unnamed types. The separation of these closely related species is difficult and requires extended field study and the comparison of living plants. The herbarium material from which many of the earlier descriptions were written is so scanty that it is almost impossible to connect it with living plants. The result is that the only way to get at the meaning of the descriptions is to visit the localities from which the original types were collected and find plants that fit the descriptions. Until this is done for practically all of the described species it is unsafe to try to characterize as new the various types which seem distinct enough as they grow.

If the second supposition is correct there are a half a dozen or so very variable species to be recognized and of course that one of each of these groups which was named first would bear the name for such species and the related later named forms would be recognized as varieties. These groups of related species are indicated in the discussion of the genera which precedes the list of species.

2. MAMILLARIA Haw.

Mostly small globose or short cylindric plants with solitary or branched stems, in one species forming large circular clusters; the surface of the stems covered with cylindrical or sometimes conical, teat-like tubercles, arranged more or less in rows but not confluent into ridges, the spines borne at the ends of the tubercles; the flowers borne in the axils of the tubercles, generally near the top of the stem, not spiny at the base; the fruit neither scaly nor spiny; seeds smooth or pitted.

Tubercles not grooved on the upper side (see *M. macromeris*).
    Central spines not present; plants quite small, generally an inch or two high and about the same in diameter, covered with very numerous, fine, white spines.
        Spines smooth; plant depressed at the top; spines of the upper tubercles often elongated, lower ones deciduous.
                1. *M. micromeris.*
        Spines minutely hairy; plant oval, sometimes branched; upper spines not elongated.
                2. *M. lasiacantha.*
    Central spines present, 1 or more.
        At least one of the central spines hooked; plants small, globose or oval, sometimes branched; spines all slender, the radials white and numerous, the centrals longer, brown or black.
            Only 1 central spine in each cluster hooked; radials 15 to 30, less than half an inch long.
                3. *M. grahami.*
            More than 1 central in some of the areolae hooked; radials 8 to 12, about the same length.
                4. *M wrightii.*
        None of the spines hooked, all of them short; centrals usually 1 (or sometimes wanting); plants flat-topped, with a thickened top-shaped root and milky sap,
            Radial spines few, 5 to 9, and stout, dull colored; central spine sometimes lacking.
                5. *M. meiacantha.*

Radial spines more numerous, 10 to 20, slender and white; centrals always present.

6. *M. heyderi.*

Tubercles grooved on the upper side (in *M. macromeris* the groove is absent in young plants and never reaches the axil), none of the spines hooked.

Central spines none or 1; plant small, subglobose, 1 to 2 inches high; radials very numerous, 30 to 50, less than half an inch long, slender.

7. *M. dasyacantha.*

Central spines several, generally 3 or more; plants larger; radial spines less numerous.

Tubercles large, mostly half an inch or more long; plants large (for the genus) with long spines.

Flowers rose purple; central spines mostly dark colored, slender but strong, generally about 2 inches long; stems usually in clusters of from 10 to 30 or more.

8. *M. macromeris.*

Flowers brownish yellow; central spines 2 to 5, light colored, stout, 1 inch long, one of them curved downward at the tip; plant mostly solitary.

9. *M. scheerii.*

Tubercles much smaller, usually about one fourth to one third of an inch long; plants small, with relatively short and numerous spines; radials mostly white.

Fruit bright red; lower spines deciduous leaving the base of the plant covered with naked tubercles which become dry and corky; spines numerous; centrals 5 to 9, purplish or ashy at the tips.

10. *M. tuberculosa.*

Fruit green; lower spines rarely deciduous; base of the stem not tuberculate; centrals mostly 4 to 6 and darker colored.

Stigmas tipped with a sharp constricted point; plant usually consisting of several clustered stems; seeds yellowish brown.

11. *M. vivipara.*

Stigmas blunt; plant usually having but one stem, though sometimes with 2 to 4; seeds reddish brown.

12. *M. radiosa.*

Two other species of Mamillaria have been reported from New Mexico but the references probably rest on the incorrect determination of specimens.

1. Mamillaria micromeris Engelm. On limestone mountains in the southeastern part of the state; in the lower sonoran zone.

2. Mamillaria lasiacantha Engelm. Known so far only from the Guadalupe Mountains west of Carlsbad, in the upper sonoran zone.

3. Mamillaria grahami Engelm. Known in New Mexico only from low mountains near Las Cruces, but to be expected further north as it occurs in Utah; our specimens from the lower sonoran zone; it probably gets into the upper sonoran also.

4. Mamillaria wrightii Engelm. Our specimens come from the mountains of the western side of the state, but it is reported from the upper Pecos region east of Santa Fe; in the upper sonoran zone.

5. Mamillaria melacantha Engelm. Occasional in the mountains of the southern part of the state in the sonoran zones.

6. Mamillaria heyderi Muhlenph. In the mountains of the southern part of the state with the preceding and more common; in the sonoran zones.

7. **Mamillaria dasyacantha** Engelm.   Rare in the mountains of the southwestern part of the state; in the upper sonoran zone. It might be mistaken for *M. micromeris* on account of its size, but its spines are different and the tubercles are grooved.

8. **Mamillaria macromeris** Engelm.   Common on the sandy mesas and plains in the southern part of the state; in the lower sonoran zone.

9. **Mamillaria scheerii** Muhlenpf.   Quite rare on the mesas and plains in the southern part of the state; in the lower sonoran zone.

10. **Mamillaria tuberculosa** Engelm.   One of the commonest of the Mamillarias, on low limestone mountains in the southern part of the state; in the sonoran zones.

11. **Mamillaria vivipara** Nutt. Known for New Mexico from a single collection high up on the Chusca mountains, in the extreme northwestern corner of the state; in the transition zone.

12. **Mamillaria radiosa** Engelm. With its varieties, it occurs almost all over the state though rarely very abundant any place; upper sonoran and transition zones.

3. ECHINOCACTUS Link and Otto.

Globose or short cylindrical plants, some of them quite large, almost universally solitary, with tubercles arranged in rows and more or less coalesced into ridges which run lengthwise of the plant or sometimes spirally part way around the stem; spines in most of the species rather stout and horny, in several they are hooked or curved; the flowers are borne just above young spine-bearing areoles, thus appearing at the centre of the plant at the top instead of at the sides: the flowers of various sizes and colors and woolly or scaly at the base, not spiny; the fruit leathery or succulent, with rather thick rind and little pulp, sometimes dry, smooth, woolly or scaly.

At least some of the spines hooked.
    Central spines 1, hooked; some of the laterals also hooked; spines slender but strong, about 4 inches long, cylindrical, straw-colored, plant smal (for the genus), about 4 inches high, slightly less in diameter.
        1. *E. uncinatus wrightii*.
    Central spines 4, stout, flattened or quadrangular, 2 to 3 inches long, (rarely 4 inches long in old specimens of one species): plant larger; up to 3 feet high or more and 1 foot in diameter.
    Central spines quadrangular, not hooked: lower radials strongly hooked.
        2. *E. cylindraceus.*
    Central spines flattened, lower one hooked; radials not hooked, merely curved.
        3. *E. wrislizeni.*
None of the spines hooked.
    Centrals 2 to 4, not stout; plants small, 4 inches high or less.
        Spines flat and flexible, papery; ridges somewhat tuberculate.
        4. *E. papyracantha.*

Spines cylindric, stiff though small; ridges continuous.

5. *E. intertextus.*

Centrals 1 or none; all spines very stout and horny: plants larger, 4 to 10 inches in diameter, though never very high.

Ribs few, 8 to 10, rounded; spines mostly cylindric; plant globose, 4 or 5 inches in diameter when mature; flowers white woolly at the base; fruit dry.

6. *E. horizonthalonius.*

Ribs more numerous, 13 to 21, more acute; spines more or less flattened; plant from 8 inches to a foot in diameter, depressed, rarely over 3 or 4 inches high; flowers not so woolly; fruit bright red and pulpy.

7. *E. texensis.*

1. Echinocactus uncinatus wrightii Engelm. Known from only a few collections in the low mountains of the southern part of the state; in the lower sonoran zone. Growing in the cactus garden.

2. Echinocactus cylindraceus Engelm. Reported by Coulter from one station in extreme western New Mexico (probably). We have not seen New Mexican material of the species.

3. Echinocactus wislizeni Engelm. Common in the southern part of the state on the mesas and near the foot of the mountains; in the lower sonoran zone. Called by its American name of "Barrel cactus" or its Mexican one of "Visnaga." Growing in the cactus garden.

4. Echinocactus papyracanthus Engelm. Originally named from material collected at Santa Fe in 1847 and reported as having been found in that region once since. We have not seen it.

5. Echinocactus intertextus Engelm. Tolerably common in the foothills of the mountains, and on the mesas of the southern part of the state; in the sonoran zones, mostly lower sonoran. Growing in the College cactus garden.

6. Echinocactus horizonthalonius Lem. On limestone ridges in the southern part of the state; in the lower sonoran zone mostly though possibly going into the upper sonoran. Growing in the College cactus garden.

7. Echinocactus texensis Hoff. Known in New Mexico only near the Texas border in the extreme southeastern part of the state in the lower (?) sonoran zone. It is called "Devil's Pincushion" in that region. Growing in the College cactus garden.

4. ECHINOCEREUS Engelmann.

Plants with globose to cylindric, solitary or sometimes much branched stems, having vertical, sometimes spiral ribs; stems from 2 inches to something like 2 feet high, from 2 to 4 inches in diameter; spine clusters on the ridges, mostly close together, so close that frequently the numerous spines overlap until the stem can hardly be seen beneath; flowers of various sizes, from less than 1 inch to 4 inches long and almost as wide when fully open, appearing on the sides of the stem near the top, but not in the middle at the top, covered with clusters of spines at the base of the flower tube, which persist on the fruit; the fruit a pulpy berry with thin greenish or reddish brown rind and numerous, small, mostly black seeds in the pleasantly acid, whitish pulp, the spines easily brushed off when the fruit is ripe.

Flowers small, less than 1 inch long, green; spines red and white.
 Radial spines, 5 to 10 mm. long; centrals 3 to 6, the lower one about 1 inch long, pointing somewhat downward; plant conical at the apex.
        1. *E. chloranthus.*
 Radial spines short, 2 to 6 mm. long, rigid, spreading at right angles to the edges of the ridges (pectinate); centrals mostly absent, occasionally a few scattered ones about an inch long; plant rounded or flattened at the apex.
        2. *E. viridiflorus.*
Flowers larger, from more than 1 to over 4 inches long, not green.
 Flowers bright yellow, large about 4 inches long, opening only in the day time, spines short, rigid, spreading (pectinate), more or less pinkish tinged.
        3. *E dasyacanthus.*
 Flowers never yellow.
  Flowers large, 2½ to 4 inches long, opening in daylight only, purple or rose color, never scarlet; petals mostly acute.
   Spines short and rigid, pectinate; centrals mostly wanting.
    Flowers purple; spines white; plants small, scarcely 2 inches high.
        4. *E. pectinatus.*
    Flowers rose colored; spines variegated red and white; plant of medium size, 4 to 8 inches tall.
        5. *E. rigidissimus.*
   Spines longer, not pectinate; centrals long and conspicuous; flowers purple.
    Spines dark colored; the upper centrals erect, curving towards each other.
        6. *E. fendleri.*
    Spines straw colored or pale yellow, very numerous and about 3 inches long, the young spines straight, dusky.
        7. *E. stramineus.*
  Flowers medium sized or small, 1¼ to about 3 inches long, (rarely a little larger,) open day and night, bright scarlet, orange scarlet, or "cardinal" red, never purple; petals mostly obtuse.
   Spines very stout, strongly angled, relatively few in each cluster.
    Spines 6 to 8, mostly 6, twisted and somewhat bent; radials ¾ to 1¼ inches long; centrals almost 2 inches long or sometimes longer.
        8. *E. gonacanthus.*
    Spines 3 to 6, mostly 3, generally shorter than in the previous species, not so strong.
        9. *E. triglochidiatus.*
   Spines more slender though rigid, mostly round, more numerous in the clusters (except in *E. paucispinus.*)
    Centrals none (sometimes 1); radials 3 to 6; spines all round or but slightly flattened, stout for the section.
        10. *E. paucispinus.*

Centrals 1 to several, mostly 3 to 5 or 6: radials 8 to 16, mostly about 10 to 13.
Centrals mostly 6: flowers small, about 1½ inches long: petals almost acute.
11. *E. neomexicanus.*
Centrals 3 to 5, mostly 4; flowers larger, 2 to 3 inches long: petals broadly obtuse.
Centrals stout and round, usually gray or pinkish gray when young, dark gray in age, ¾ to 2 inches long.
12. *E. polyacanthus.*
Centrals more slender, yellowish gray or darker.
Spines shorter, mostly yellowish, centrals from a little more than half an inch to 1¾ inches long; plant rounded or somewhat depressed at the apex.
13. *E. coccineus.*
Spines longer, mostly dark colored; centrals 1 to almost 3 inches long, commonly about 2 inches; plant conical at the apex.
14. *E. conoideus.*

Two other species have been reported from New Mexico, but we have not seen anything from New Mexico which could be properly referred to them. One of them, *E. hexaedrus* Engelm., is probably only another and later name for *E. gonacanthus* which comes from the same region where it is fairly common. What the other plant may be, which Dr. Coulter refers to *E. octacanthus* (based on a specimen from Santa·Fe) we are unable to say certainly.

1. Echinocereus chloranthus (Engelm.) Rumpl. In the drier mountains of the southern part of the state; in the sonoran zones.

2. Echinocereus viridiflorus Engelm. On the high plains and in the mountain foothills, almost throughout the state; in the upper sonoran zone. Not yet collected on the western side of the state.

3. Echinocereus dasyacanthus Engelm. Known only from the extreme southeastern part of the state; in the sonoran zones.

4. Echinocereus pectinatus (Schiedw.) Engelm. Known only from the southeastern part of the state on the plains; in the lower sonoran zone.

5. Echinocereus rigidissimus (Engelm.) Rose. "Rainbow cactus." Known only from the extreme southwestern part of the state; in the sonoran zones.

6. Echinocereus fendleri (Engelm.) Rumpl. In the lower part of the mountains almost everywhere in the state; in the upper sonoran zone.

7. Echinocereus stramineus (Engelm.) Rumpl. Low limestone mountains of the southern half of the state; in the lower sonoran zone.

8. Echinocereus gonacanthus (Engelm. & Bigel.) Lem. Scattered pretty widely over the state; in the sonoran zones, though never abundant in any place.

9. **Echinocereus triglochidiatus** Engelm. In the region about Santa Fe and northward; in the upper sonoran zone.

10. **Echinocereus paucispinus** (Englem.) Rumpl. In the northern part of the state; in the upper sonoran zone.

11. **Echinocereus neo mexicanus** Standley. Known only from the mesas near Agricultural College; in the lower sonoran zone.

12. **Echinocereus polyacanthus** Engelm. On the mesas and in the mountains of the southern part of the state; in the lower sonoran zone.

13. **Echinocereus coccineus** Engelm. In the mountains, and to some extent on the mesas, almost throught the state; in the upper sonoran zone.

14. **Echinocereus conoideus** (Engelm. & Bigel.) Rumpl. In the same situations and frequently with the preceding; in the upper sonoran zone.

5. PENIOCEREUS Rose.

Slender, more or less prismatic (mostly 4-angled) stems 1 or 2 feet high, sparingly branched, arising from a large beet-like or spindle shaped tuberous root 6 inches to 1 foot in length and 2 to 4 inches in diameter; spines very short, about $\frac{1}{16}$ of an inch long or a little more, with a swelled base, few in each cluster, rather stout, arranged rather close together along the angles of the stem; flower long funnel-shaped, six inches long or more, with slender white petals, opening only one night, its base not spiny; fruit tipped with the dried and bent tube of the flower, more or less recurved.

There is but a single species of the genus found in our range and it is nowhere common.

1. **Peniocereus greggii** (Engelm.) Rose. The "Deer's-horn Cactus" has been found but twice in New Mexico so far, in the southern part of the state; in the lower sonoran zone.

ECHINOCEREUS CONOIDEUS.

ECHINOCEREUS COCCINEUS.

ECHINOCERUS GONACANTHEUS.

OPUNTIA TENUISPINA.   Badly attacked by cochineal.

OPUNTIA DULCIS.   Showing heavily fruited joint.

OPUNTIA DULCIS.   In fruit.

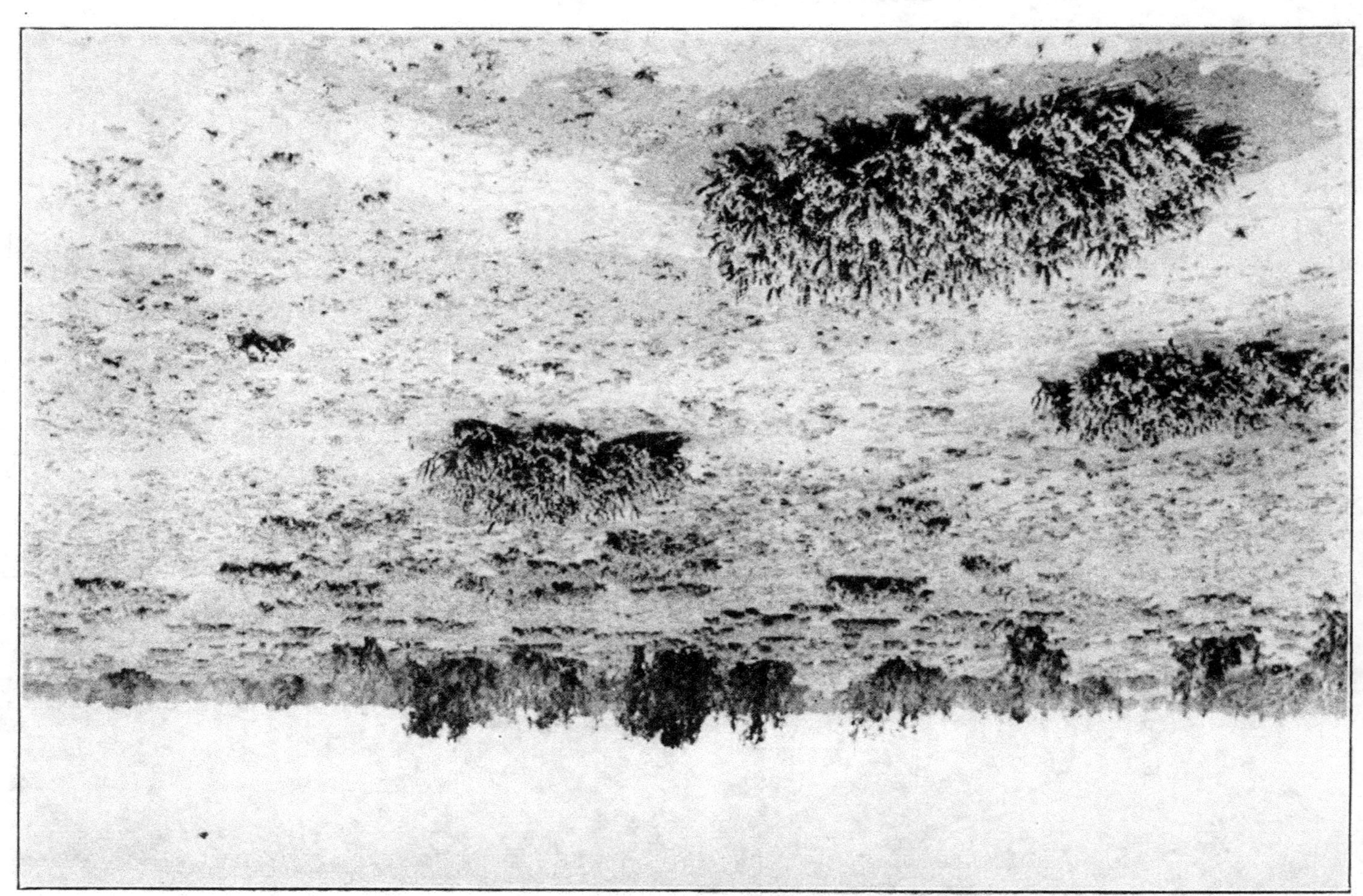

OPUNTIA WHIPPLEI. Showing habit.

OPUNTIA WHIPPLEI. Near View. The rule is four inches long.

OPUNTIA ARBORESCENS

OPUNTIA EMORYI.

OPUNTIA MACROCENTRA.

OPUNTIA CHIHUAHUAENSIS.

OPUNTIA ENGELMANNI. In fruit.

OPUNTIA ENGELMANNI.

OPUNTIA CHLOROTICA.

OPUNTIA POLYACANTHA.

www.ingramcontent.com/pod-product-compliance
Lightning Source LLC
Chambersburg PA
CBHW081625250726
48657CB00009B/2723